Communicating Love
Through Prayer

Communicating Love
Through Prayer

By
Rosalind Rinker

Zondervan Publishing House
Grand Rapids, Michigan

First printing........May, 1966
Second printing....October, 1966
Third printing.......July, 1967
Fourth printing ....August, 1967
Fifth printing.......March, 1968
Sixth printing....November, 1968

Library of Congress catalog card number: 66-18940

Quotations from *The New English Bible,* New Testament, © The Delegates of the Oxford University Press and The Syndics of the Cambridge University Press, 1961, are reprinted by permission.

Quotations from J. B. Phillips, *The New Testament in Modern English,* The Macmillan Company, copyright © 1958 by J. B. Phillips, are used by permission of the publisher.

The quotation from Reuel L. Howe, *Herein Is Love,* The Judson Press, 1961, is used by permission of the publisher.

Printed in the United States of America

To
Major Carol M. Williams
United States Air Force
My Christian Friend
Editor
and
Faithful Critic

Preface

Since writing my first book on prayer five years ago, I've discovered that if we are to fully cooperate and follow the prayer-teachings of our Lord, He needs our minds plus our imaginations.

If we could only be as little children, we could respond to God without fear, and learn to pray with one another as a means of communicating love. Communication lines need to be opened and to be kept open. Only when they are, do life and personality assume deeper meaning.

I would like to express my appreciation to Floyd W. Thatcher, Zondervan Publishing House, for his constant encouragement during the time this manuscript was being written.

To Major Carol M. Williams, United States Air Force, I am especially grateful for giving valuable time to editing this manuscript (as well as one of my previous books). Major Williams taught me, by example, the meaning of hard work and good craftsmanship in writing. Though our viewpoints sometimes differ, the lively discussions over topics in this book fostered clearer thinking and more explicit writing.

ROSALIND RINKER

Chicago, Illinois
September, 1965

CONTENTS

Part I. Love, Prayer and Communication

～1～

Prayer—what does it communicate?

Prayer, communication and love are so closely linked together in everyday life that to omit any one of them is to become a spiritual cripple.

"Communicating love? What's that about?" a lady asked when she saw the title of this book.

"It's about God," I answered, "and how much He loves us. It's about us . . . and how we can love one another."

Do you believe God loves you?

If you do, you won't have any trouble at all answering this lady's question. If you don't really believe God loves you, you'll hesitate and hedge a bit, or you'll come right out and say, "Me? how could He love me?" In either case, your answer will show that you do not accept yourself, nor do you know how great is the heart of God.

Being who He is, God's love is unconditional. Therefore He can accept us, forgive us, and love us as we are.

Love's nature is to communicate. There are countless ways to communicate, and however unsatisfactory it may be, speech is one of them. To speak with God is called *prayer,* a religious practice from which many, although deeply religious in spirit, shy away. We need a simpler approach to prayer which will attract and not repel.

To learn to pray

To learn to pray is to learn to love. Prayer is a dialogue

between two people who love each other, because
prayer is the language of the heart.

Have you ever listened to yourself pray, like a third
party listening in? Did you ever try to "edit" your prayers,
to find out exactly what you are saying?

When you pray, do you say what your heart wants to
say? Or, ignoring your heart, do you pray for the ears
of people? When did you last listen to what your heart
was saying?

It is a wonderfully freeing experience to get your
mouth and your heart together, to say what you mean
and mean what you say, and come to the point. Well,
why not? It makes good sense, doesn't it?

Listen next time you or another is asked to pray —
whether for giving thanks at a meal, or opening a Sunday
school class, or at family prayers, or wherever. Why pray
just to get it over with? Why pray with "clichés" which
have outworn their meaning? Who listens to this kind
of praying? Why be so general and so inclusive that
there is no interest at all in what is being said?

Prayer should be an outbreathing of the love which
God Himself has put into you. Prayer should be speaking
with God, for He is present and loves not only you but
also your brother. Essentially, prayer should be simple,
expressing straightforward gratitude or asking for what
we need at that particular time. The past may need
confession, while the future calls for trust.

In group prayer, the prayer which truly communicates
is the prayer expressing love. When someone so prays, I
am loved. So are you. So is everyone present.

Prayer that contains the power of reaching from one
to another, the power to heal and to make whole through
the giving and receiving of love, is real prayer. This

means more than speech. It means giving one's self to others all day long in love, because Jesus Christ, the author of love, is already there in your inner being. Every act and thought can be prayer, projected by the choice to love.

To love

The greatest need of any human being is love. God made us like this. Our trouble is that we confuse different kinds of love until we may think God rejects us because some person has rejected us. The quality of God's love is of a different essence from human love, even though all human love must of necessity spring from Him who is the source.

To most people love means sex and possession. No wonder we are so soon disillusioned. Love is openly sought by youth. Older people settle for security and companionship, but nevertheless long for love.

To love is imperative. We must love or perish. But we must love with an unselfish love, a giving love, the kind of love God gives to us, the kind of love that involves us with each other — in time, in words, in caring. Yet because we are human and cannot read one another's minds, loving us makes us vulnerable. We can be hurt, misunderstood and rejected. And we in turn will hurt others with or without "malice aforethought."

The big problem, as I see it, is that we cannot love each other for the simple reason we don't love ourselves! And how can we love ourselves, until we are certain that God loves us? But when we know that He does indeed love us, then everything changes! Then we can tell it, and others listening will believe us, because they know we are speaking from the heart and from personal experience.

In a recent meeting a lady asked me, "Have you ever been married?" The group of 60 waited for my answer. I stood speechless for a moment, never having been put on the spot like this in a public gathering. Then the answer came to me, as it always does when I wait for it.

"No, I haven't, but it isn't my fault!" The laughter which followed drew us together dispelling the loneliness which up to that moment all had felt.

"How is it," asked another, "that never having been married you nevertheless understand all of our problems?"

Well, I haven't exactly been a hermit all my life. I've lived in China and among students, and travelled widely. I have eyes and ears, and a heart with which to give and receive love. And single or married, everyone has problems, everyone has a sense of aloneness which must be recognized, accepted and utilized. In a sense, everyone lives alone. This is why we all need to learn to communicate and to love.

Communicating love can be done by prayer. And we can all learn to pray. When love is poured right into the words being said, God becomes more real and is more often felt to be present. This is because love is His gift to our hearts. God is love, He gives us Himself, and we are loved.

What then do we do with love? We misuse it right and left. We hoard it selfishly. We bottle it up in business, houses, lands, cars, possessions, and seldom share it with anyone. But if it is to grow, love must be given away. Love given away increases in depth and in quality. When we give love to one another in any manner acceptable to each other, we are communicating. We are not communicating when our own ideas of giving love take precedence. We *are* communicating when we serve one another in love.

We are communicating the most important message in all the world when we say (having first believed it ourselves) *God is love. God loves you; yes, you.* Do you believe it? **Can** you say it? Say it now and believe it.

This is the message the world is waiting to **hear** — that God **loves** sinners, and *this sinner* in particular. God is love and God offers forgiveness — for you and for me and for all who, hearing His invitation, will come.

To communicate

Later (in Chapter 11) I will discuss communication and will link it with God, love and prayer. I want to put it into a personal setting where there are words which the heart longs to hear, words of love and invitation, words of acceptance and response that break down walls of fear and open doors of shared joy. When doors are open, then the breakdown in communication — between husband and wife, between parents and children, between friends, between all peoples — will be and can be healed and restored. The hard heart will be softened, the rebellious won, the hungry fed, the searching will find, the doubting will believe. The heart will be at peace in shared love.

Such love and understanding can be found when we are together in the Presence of God — in God who has revealed Himself through Jesus Christ, the Lord of life, the Lord of love, the Lord of all creation.

God is speaking all the time. Who is ready to respond to the Voice of Love — the love of God speaking to us . . . through us? But not until we have first learned to listen are we ready to respond.

Communication is an essential word in today's world. We hear it everywhere. But how and to what degree are we personally involved with it? A lack of communication may well be the basis for personal unhappiness, racial distress, political disagreement — from divorce to cold wars. When the communication of love has been established, there is greater potential for peace, progress, integration, and meaning to life, for individuals, for families, for cities, and for nations.

Communicating love is always possible when God is present.

And God *is* always present!

⌐

God is speaking all the time, all the time, all the time.
—*Frank Laubach.*

⌐

Suggestions for study

1. As you go through the chapter again, write down short sentences which express the nature of God's love.
2. Think about these words in relation to why prayer may be dull. Supply a creative word as the opposite for the following:

repetitious	general
impersonal	traditional
habitual	clichés
too inclusive	non-communicative

3. List a few reasons why you believe communication has broken down between you and another.
4. "Hitherto have ye asked nothing in my name; ask, and ye shall receive, that your joy may be full" (John 16:24). Memorize this verse.

⌐

~2~

How can I know God loves me?

In this chapter, seven people tell how they learned to know God loves them, personally.

One of my great discoveries in the life of prayer — which is communicating with God — is the simple fact that God loves people. Good or bad, strong or weak, young or old, rich or poor, black or white, He loves them all. I had to discover that His love included me regardless of whether I considered myself good or bad.

"I don't believe God loves me," declared a young woman from the back seat of a car in which we were riding. I turned and looked at her, for it was the first time I'd ever heard anyone make such a statement. She had, I learned, experienced an unhappy and bitter childhood. The early treatment to which she had been subjected had so inhibited her, she was unable either to accept love or to express love.

Since then I've met others like her. Their reactions always seem to involve a parent unable to give love to the child. Rejection and an accompanying lack of love-security is expressed in a person's face. It shows in the set of the mouth, and is often revealed by bitten finger-nails and nervous gestures.

Do you know and believe God's love for you?

19

Do you ever say to yourself when you arise in the morning, "A new day! God loves me! Thank You, Father!" When you walk do you lift up your head, and let the smile on your face show God and others you're glad? When you truly learn the magnitude of God's personal love and concern for you, then your entire being can and should reflect the joy of being alive, the happiness of being loved.

Since my discovery that God really loves each of us regardless of what we may think of ourselves, I've tried to help others make this same discovery.

Because of what they've done, think they are, or have become, many people can't believe God loves them. Often these people cannot love themselves, let alone others. They consider themselves hypocrites because of the false front they feel forced to display before the world.

Nevertheless it is true. God loves them. And Jesus loves them.

⌐

"Thank you for showing me Jesus loves me," wrote a friend. "Not only me, but everyone. I guess I never realized He loves people just the way they are. Now I'm looking at everyone I meet through different eyes. Now it seems so right to say in my heart (as I look at others), 'God loves you, and so do I.' "

Another wrote: "That morning you spoke, you repeated over and over, *God loves you, just as you are.* I saw Christ in you, loving me. It was so new to me, I couldn't forget it. A few months later my heart was completely open, and I met Christ as my personal Saviour."

Still another: "I guess it's because I've never been able to accept myself, nor feel others would accept me, that I believed I was not good enough to be accepted by Christ. I have asked Him to come into my life, but I never felt loved. How could He love me, when I don't love myself? You were so convincing, when you said Jesus loved *me*. It was when we were sitting in that car, and you mentioned how Christ loved the different people who passed by, and how everyone meant so much to Him no matter who they are, or what they do . . . it was then I realized that in spite of all my weakness, He wanted to give me His love too. The love I have since received from Him has been wonderful."

A brilliant woman in Honolulu came to see me one day. The first thing she said was, "Now, tell me what God is like." So well-masked was her quiet desperation, I couldn't have chosen a better place to start than by answering her question.

"Probably not what you think He's like, and certainly not at all like many so-called Christians." She was so relieved — the tension left her and she began to relax. Our conversation continued over a period of time, during which she discovered God had not stopped loving her simply because factors in her own life and conduct made her believe He no longer cared.

People remember and hold things against themselves. People remember and hold things against each other. God, however, casts all our sins into the deepest sea, the sea of His forgetfulness. Corrie ten Boom, author and speaker, says, "And we should put up a sign, *no fishing!*" This means also, *no diving,* because once God has forgiven us it is a sin against His love for us to either bring up our own or the sins of others.

"I attended one of your recent prayer workshops," wrote M.D. of Ohio, "and left with a great blessing. We have your record album and have used it in prayer meetings where it was not only enthusiastically received but helped many to revitalize their prayer life. I never before really felt God's love. I had trusted Him as my Saviour but wondered why my heart seemed so cold. Now that I understand His love and respond to it, I'm able to share it with others. Instead of carrying my own burdens and nearly breaking under the load (because I thought God sent them) I'm beginning to turn them over to Him."

The personal experiences and discoveries just related may not convince some of you. You probably consider your problems uniquely different. But they aren't really. And even if they were, God still understands them. It's your heart, not your mind, which needs reassuring before you can solve them. When your heart is assured of God's love for you, your mind will become convinced. Make the latter receptive and assurance will follow. All it takes is your cooperation.

Making my own discovery

I once believed God loved only those who obeyed Him — that He punished all others.

As a young Christian, John 14:21 was one of the first Scripture verses I memorized. The emphasis it places upon love given as a result of obedience profoundly influenced my thinking. I reasoned that when I was good and obedient I was loved; when I was disobedient (willfully so, or accidentally so) I was rejected and unloved. Consequently I became increasingly adept at rationalization. I didn't want to think of myself as unloved by God. Further, I uncon-

sciously began to view all unbelievers as outside the realm
of God's love.

The day came when I awoke to the realization that
I didn't really love people at all. I thought all Christians
were like myself — putting on a good "face" for the
world to see. I thought all non-Christians were in a
sorry state without God's love and I didn't love them
either!

Paul Tournier's book, *The Meaning of Persons* (Harper,
1957), helped me to accept myself as I am. Only then
did God's love become personal for me. Dr. Tournier
writes: "Integration is not at all a simplification of the
mind. On the contrary it is a progressive realization of
one's secret propensities, and a lucid and courageous
acceptance of the totality of one's being, with all its
complications and contradictions" (p. 61).

A further contribution was made to my need when
a Christian in all kindness asked a simple question: *For
how many of your sins did Christ die?* In a flash I saw
the truth: Why, for all of them — past, present, future!
Before I ever sinned a single sin, Christ died for me.
His death and resurrection were God's way of saying,
"You're mine now. I've taken care of your guilt and your
sin. That's how much I love you." Love like this assured
me of acceptance as well as forgiveness. Even my Bible
became a new book as I searched it with newly opened
eyes.

At once I was able to accept others and love them,
good or bad, Christian or non-Christian. Being loved
by God and knowing what to do with sin and failure
(i.e. Jesus Christ has already carried them all for me),
I could with authority say to any person on earth: *God*

loves you. I could say it because I knew He loved and accepted me, and because it is true.

The day I began to more fully comprehend God's love for people I was driving an old car from California to Idaho. The catch on the hood was damaged and the wind kept pulling the hood up in the air. I stopped again and again to tie it down, but there was a refrain going on in my heart and mind all day long, over and over. It rang when I passed a farm house or a tractor crossing a half-plowed field; it sang as I passed other cars, or drove through small towns.

"I wonder if the people living there know God loves them. Do they know how much God loves them? God loves you, sir. God loves you. I wonder if you know that God loves you."

I didn't know them, would never meet them nor speak to them face-to-face. But one thing I did know: God loved each one of them. Jesus died for them. He longed for them to know this. To the extent they didn't know, they were both spiritually blind and crippled.

All the while I was driving north I literally felt God's love flowing into me and enabling me to let it pour out from my own heart in an ever-widening river of love for others.

Someone may still ask, "Does God really love the disobedient?"

What about the children you know? Aren't they both obedient and disobedient in one single day? Do parents stop loving them when they are naughty? No, and neither does God. He loves us, His children, in whatever state we may be. In every situation we can think of, His love remains constant. Read Romans 8:31-39 in the New

English Bible for one of the most powerful passages in the Scriptures concerning God's love.

"Thank you," wrote a friend, "for giving me a clearer picture of Christ's love. Even when I fight and kick and try with all my might to run away, He never gives up on me. He just goes on loving me. His love is the most powerful weapon in the world. He always conquers me with love — and I can be pretty touchy sometimes! But like you, I belong to Him and I'm His forever."

Christ's life on earth revealed His love and mercy and kindness, for people who had lost their way and knew it. His severity was for those false at heart.

I have a new appreciation for the story of the prodigal son — with whom I would never have been caught associating (notice the past tense) — ever since I discovered the reason Jesus told it. Read the 15th chapter of Luke. To the religious people, who drew their skirts away from sinners and criticized Jesus for keeping such company, He told three stories. I wonder if they ever got the point!

I think I love the story of the lost sheep best of all — that foolish, not-meaning-to-get-lost sheep who just wandered and wandered until he was hopelessly confused and alone. How eager, how anxious is the shepherd! Listen! He is calling, waiting, searching until He finds it. There! He gently lifts it to His shoulders, holding it close to Himself, caressing and talking quietly until it stops trembling. See with what delight and joy He takes it home with Him!

This is what God is like.

This is how Jesus loves you.

Then Jesus tells of the lost coin, over which the owner

mourned until she found it, whereupon there was great joy.

Lastly, He relates the story of the lost son— that son who purposefully and willfully got lost, but whose father was waiting, longing, hoping for his return. In these three stories there is joy and also rejoicing.

Each of these stories tells us what God is really like, because God reveals Himself in Jesus Christ. They tell us what we are like and what He intends to do about us: *love us and find us!*

Can God love us as we are?

Indeed yes! He loves us just as we are!

How can you believe it?

Be willing to change your mental attitude about Jesus Christ, and about yourself.

Be willing to consent to let Him love you even if you consider yourself unworthy.

This is belief.

This is faith.

Your response makes the gift yours.

What are you waiting for?

Make your answer honest.

Prayer is your heart
responding
to the fact of God's love.

Review and study questions

1. How does God convince people that He loves them?
2. Discuss: What God is like — His nature. The life and death of Christ as a basis for personally accepting His love.

3. Study the following Scriptures to learn that God's love and blessing are not wages which we've earned, but gifts beyond all we deserve: Ephesians 1:5, 6; 2:4-10. Romans 3:23-28; 5:5-11; 8:31-39. Matthew 5:45; 7:7-11. I Corinthians 2:9-12. I Peter 2:22-25. John 10:27-30.

4. What you put into words soon becomes truth for you. Try this experiment using the following:
God loves you. Jesus loves you. And I love you. Tell God that whenever these words come to your mind, you will express them. Then do it. You can do it silently as you look at another. You can do it audibly if it seems right. If you don't think of it, you obviously can't do it. If you do remember — know that God is there, reminding you, reaching for you, caring for you — and for others through you.

Part II.   Attitudes Which Need Healing

∽3∽

We could hear . . . if
only we'd listen

I think it probably all started the day I had my first ride in a jet plane. So smooth. So silent. With so much sudden power we slipped up through the air. Then, there we were — 36,000 feet above the earth's surface.

Looking down I felt almost like an astronaut. Then involuntarily and immediately my mind switched gears and I felt more like an ant! Why, from that height I couldn't even see one human being! They were down there all right — I'd just come from there and would soon be going back. But all I could see that made sense was the broad face of the earth, with its checkered fields and forests, and here or there a lake, a river, a highway. Clouds? Well, yes, they were there, but so far, far down they looked like clumps of cotton batting stuck on the scenery.

I was suddenly almost drowned in a torrent of questions which seemed to come from within:

Does it really matter what happens down there?

Does it matter what happens to you? Or to anyone? You can't see anyone from here.

Nobody knows, maybe God doesn't even know, who's there. From here, you can't see anyone.

Pretty small, eh? You . . . and the rest of them.

Lots of them, too. Hundreds. Thousands. Millions.

From here, who knows what's going on?

How can God tell you apart?

You're just like a million ants, can't tell one from an-other (the questions went on and on). *All huddling, hur-rying, burrowing, scurrying, collecting. And for what? Number one first. Get what you want, that's it. What else? And who cares about the have-nots? or their dis-tresses and privations? or the guilty and their fears? or the sick and imprisoned and their needs?*

Does God care? You thought He did, didn't you? How can He, when He's so big and you're so small? And this earth — it's only one infinitesimal speck of His immense universe.

Now, that little town — do you think God really cares about what goes on down there? About who goes where? Who belongs to whom, and to what? Who sleeps where, and with whom? Who is well and who isn't? Who does good and who does evil? Who has houses and lands and cars and money and who has none? Does God care? Does God care who has loved ones to come home to and who has no one to come home to? Does God care about that?

Relentlessly my thoughts continued. I sat motionless. Maybe some of it was true — or partly true. It wasn't all true, because God isn't like this — even if we are.

The questions went on: *Isn't He? Isn't He your Father in heaven? Your heavenly Father? Your Father up here in the heavens?*

Yes, but . . . I began to resist consciously now, and to counter in self-defense, in order to keep the flood of ques-tions from penetrating any deeper. They hurt enough as it was. Yes . . . but our Father is like Jesus Christ, and

Jesus Christ is the Good Shepherd who always cares for His own.

With the saying of His name, even within my mind, came a miracle. He was there! The Good Shepherd Himself was there with me. Of course! I remembered the story of *Hind's Feet* (by Hannah Hurnard). This is a kind of feminine *Pilgrim's Progress*, in which the little pilgrim (who went on a long journey to find love) was given one effective weapon to use whenever her enemies came upon her in any form. All she had to do was to say the name of the Good Shepherd, and He would be there, present with her, to protect and to comfort her. Otherwise, she journeyed seemingly alone, without the visible presence of her Shepherd.

It worked too, when she said His Name — He was there! What worked for the little pilgrim, now worked for me. Worked so well I felt not only the presence of the Good Shepherd, but heard His voice in my heart.

— Yes, I *am* here, Ros. With you and within you. Remember?

It was my Shepherd's voice. I'd heard Him before. I knew His voice. I listened. I could almost feel His hands there upon my shoulders. I hoped He'd say more — there must be more. There was more.

— I'm right here. I've been here all the time. You know this. Even if you forget Me for a while, I never forget you — not for one instant.

— Now, about all those black-bordered statements and questions. I heard them, but they were not from Me. Only those whose spirits are sick, or those who have never learned to listen take any stock at all in such evil and doubt-filled ideas. You have to look and look again intently at things intangible, for they are not what they may appear.

— I am your Shepherd, your Lord. Do I ever change?

One of the Bible verses I learned years ago flashed through my mind: "Jesus Christ, the same, yesterday and today, and forever" (Hebrews 13:8).

His voice went on.

— I'm just the same up here in this plane as I am when I'm down there with you. Exactly the same. Aren't you? You're the same person sitting here in this jet as the person you are down there. What difference does it make where you are? You are you.

⌐

That did it. I was I, and He was He. It was that simple. Wherever we were, whatever we did, He changes not.

The words of a hymn I love came back to me.

> The clouds may come and go
> And storms may sweep my sky,
> This blood-seal'd friendship changes not:
> The cross is ever nigh.
>
> My love is oft-times low,
> My joy still ebbs and flows;
> But peace with Him remains the same
> No change Jehovah knows.
>
> I change, He changes not,
> The Christ can never die
> His love, not mine, the resting place,
> His truth, not mine, the tie.
>
> I hear the words of love,
> I gaze upon the blood,
> I see the mighty sacrifice
> And I have peace with God.

'Tis everlasting peace!
Sure as Jehovah's Name;
'Tis stable as His steadfast throne,
For evermore the same.

—*Horatius Bonar.*

Meditation No. 1

1. Read Jeremiah 31:3.
2. Reread the poem again at the end of the chapter, as a prayer.
3. Try repeating in a thankful attitude, with as many varying forms as you can, these words: Jesus is here.
4. Go through the italics and pick out all the hidden truths about God, giving thanks for each one. (In order to make them acceptable, communications coming from the Power of Evil are masked with an element of truth.)

Prayer is knowing that Jesus is there and cares.

⟶4⟵

We could hear . . . if we
weren't afraid

Listening to God can be disturbing and unsettling for it often involves change — change in attitude, in relationships, change in vocation or location. Anything could change if we got lined up with God's best plan for us, if we stopped long enough for the tumult to die down, to get quiet enough to hear God speak. Particularly if we weren't afraid of what He might have to say to us.

How does God speak to us? He speaks to us through our past. He speaks to us in our present situation. And He speaks to us through our own arguments, through our fears and failures, through His love, through other people, books, pain and suffering. He speaks to us by every possible means at every possible time.

"But how can you tell," asked one of my friends, willing to argue a little, "whether it is God speaking or whether you're just listening to your own thoughts?"

I just talk to Him. "Lord, are You saying this to me? If you are, I want to do it. Keep on speaking to me, so I'll know for sure. If You aren't and it comes from some other source, let it be like water poured on the ground — don't let it come back to me at all."

I've also learned to watch my own reactions. When I start to argue with myself, I can be pretty sure that God is speaking and that what I'm doing is trying to protect myself. So, I refer it all back to the One who loves me. Deep in my heart I am surrendered to His whole will. I've already said *Yes, Lord* to all of life. My surrender only needs to be worked out in each instance. He knows this, and I know He knows. So I ask Him, confident He will answer.

I'll admit it is sometimes difficult to know if God is really giving me directions. However, after some experimenting, I realize God has control of my mind, and because He loves me, He will get through to me. Often, looking back it is easier to see how God has led me in the past. So I move out, take the risk of faith and trust Him. Afterward, I can quietly state God did speak to me, lead me, and safely hold me.

One has to be careful, however, about stating, "God told me to do this." That statement smacks of self-confidence and pride. Be quiet, walk softly, move ahead slowly, and do what you believe in your own heart He asks you to do. Afterwards you can tell it all with joy.

There is one infallible test: Is what is coming through to me — love? Is love communicating? Will this make me love God more or less? Will it prove that I love my brother unselfishly, that I am eager for his good? Love protects. Love sets free.

Floyd W. Thatcher, my Zondervan editor, gave me a test which works for him. "Am I being pushed or guided? Time will tell. Time will take care of this. If it is personal desire, it won't stand the test of time. If it is God speaking, then it doesn't matter if I wait one day, one week or one month." Chapters 3, 4, 5 of my book *You Can Witness With Confidence* tell some of my early experiences in self-occupation, compulsion and learning to wait.

Then there is always the test of God's Word. I will never be asked to do something contrary to His will. If what has been suggested to me is God's will, doors will be opened to help make it possible.

The voice of love

When God, who loves you, wants to communicate with you, where does He start? This depends on you. If you haven't yet responded to Him, the first thing He wants is to establish a personal relationship with you. God is interested in everything which concerns you. To get your attention may require a few changes on your part, which He will engineer without consulting you. But He will wait until you are ready, and you will find readiness becoming evident in more ways than one. This too, is His love.

What about you? What if God did speak to you? Would you be afraid to listen? Then you really do have reservations about His love, don't you? You needn't, for one of the proofs of love is the desire to establish communication.

When we think of speaking with someone we love, we usually picture ourselves talking face to face, even though we use the telephone and the letter. One thing is sure, no dialogue is lacking when two people love each other. Dialogue is incomplete only when one person reaches out and the other fails to respond.

"The purpose of dialogue," says Reuel Howe in his book, *The Miracle of Dialogue* (p. 66, Seabury), "is the calling forth of persons in order that they may be united (or reunited) with one another, know the truth, and love God, man and themselves."

The first time I remember God speaking to me was through the voice of another who invited me to give my heart to Christ. My response helped to bring about this new relationship, and as a result I became a new person, called forth to unfold and to develop as a child of God. I stopped trying to plan my own life, and I put myself into His hands.

As a teen-ager, my prayer was, "Lord, what do You want me to do with my life?"

The next time God's love and voice came to me, it was through a book. I was reading the life story of J. Hudson Taylor, the founder of the China Inland Mission. As I read some of his experiences with the Chinese, I was amazed that they were people like myself, not heathen unlike me! My heart became involved, and I loved them.

The only talent I thought I possessed was the ability to talk and tell something so people would believe it. From within the calling Voice seemed to say, "Follow Me. Leave your homeland, parents, brothers and sisters, friends, and go to China — where you can share the love of Christ." There was both pain and joy in the struggle to respond to the Voice. There was pain as in my mind I said good-bye and seemed to embark on a big white ship for China. (It did turn out to be a big white ship — the *S. S. Empress of Canada.*) And there was gladness because God had spoken, because He had a plan for me, and He had made some of it known to me.

The voice we fear

Listening to God speak brings ultimate joy and gladness. Why, then, are we afraid to listen? Self-protection for one thing. For another, the possibility that the voice does not belong to God. Jesus gives us teaching on the voices His sheep listen to, in the 10th chapter of John.

There is a healthy kind of fear which makes us aware of danger when the thief is near. There is an unhealthy kind of fear that almost makes us shut God out — like the voices on that jet.

"Did you actually hear voices on that jet?" asked one who heard me tell the experience.

Rather than come right out and say, "Of course not," my answer was, "Do you know you have more than two ears? You have a third ear in your heart. Everyone has, only most of us are afraid to use it."

The devotional material at the close of Chapter 3 quickly provides a clue to the positive truths contained in my experience in that jet plane. Satan designed them to make me question God. Such communications are never love-oriented. And indeed there was no love communicating in those suggestions. By their very nature and content they had the unmistakable aroma of their author: *Doubt God and run your own life.*

People have asked me after teaching sessions why I seldom mention Satan's name. "He's smarter than I am, so I let Jesus Christ take care of him. I don't want any direct dealings with him. Nor do I wish to give him the satisfaction of addressing him, or using his name."

Yet we cannot hide behind the lame excuse that we might be obeying Satan rather than God. If we really want to listen and hear God's voice, we will remember that Jesus said, "My sheep know my voice and they follow Me."

Neither should we ignore this enemy from darkness or be unaware of his general tactics. They are the same as of old — in the Garden of Eden —questioning God's purpose, doubting God's love, throwing up a smoke screen to eliminate the possibility of any guided, creative thinking in alignment with God's will.

Did God really say it? Does God really mean it? These are the kinds of questions the Devil (by whatever name he is called) uses, including such suggestions as: *Why not use your own mind and figure it out? Run your own life, that's why He gave you the ability you have.*

I can usually recognize this voice by the subtle attempt to blend truth and error which begins to show up in selfish plans, failure to consider others, and fear to make any change in the status quo.

Let's face it. We are afraid.

Years ago, while on vacation in California, I remember hearing Dr. E. Stanley Jones for the first time. He made the following statement: "You are never safe until you can stand the worst possible thing that could happen to you." For a long time I was unable to accept this statement, for I could not face the fear within me. Before long the fear I feared came to pass: I loved someone whom I could not have. Then I learned that dread can be taken out of fear and turned into faith when it is shared with Jesus Christ — faith in His love, His plan, His care, His Presence.

Why do we always resist change? Change is the order of the day in our present world. Yet we want things the way we want them, to go on as they once did. Is it because we don't like to admit either to ourselves or others that we were wrong, that we've been stubborn and dogmatic and need to change?

Change is often an affront to us. We cling to the bit of security we've made for ourselves, knowing we can never recapture the past and that the future is beyond our power to control anyway.

To summarize: We must listen to God, who loves us and cares for us. He wants to give us only the very best, but to do so He needs our daily cooperation that we may receive all the gifts which He so much desires for us.

⌐

Things to remember:

1. All the ways in which God speaks to us. List them.
2. The tests which can help us to be certain that God is speaking.
3. The reasons for fear. Can you add some more?
4. Results of hearing God speak to us.

⌐

Meditation No. 2

Read: Psalm 139
Subject: God Cares

1. Verse by verse, give thanks for each part of God's care for you. Where is He not to be found?
2. Face up to all the things you are afraid of. Face the fear you fear the most. Imagine it coming to pass. Try to live through it in your imagination. What would it mean to you? In words, now commit the whole situation, actual and possible to God who knows all hearts and who loves you.
3. Give thanks that His love will only permit what, in the end, is best for all. Read Romans 8:28.

⌐

~5~

We could listen . . . if we were willing

We could all listen to God speaking if we really wanted to. What miracles could take place if only we would listen! Learning to listen is part of learning to pray — for only then can we be instructed and *know* we are loved. Only by listening can we be capable of becoming the whole person God intended us to be.

Following the two instances of listening to God mentioned in the last chapter, and after God had taken care of two important areas in my life, I felt quite secure. Early in my second term in China, though, to my dismay I found God had not finished speaking.

I was still a very young missionary and had not yet discovered that prayer is a dialogue between two people who love one another and trust one another. For me, prayer was a monologue, a one-way conversation. I prayed until I finished. Now — I'm never finished! There is a joyous dialogue which goes on forever.

An open ear needs to be kept open. But keeping it open requires both discipline and obedience. Otherwise, do you know what happens? We simply coast along with nothing new, nothing fresh, until God with infinite love and patience succeeds in regaining our attention.

Looking back, I realize my Christian life had increasingly consisted of things I did or did not do, depending upon the theological dictates of our church and beliefs to which it did or did not subscribe. While in no way depreciating the importance of these, it took me years to "separate the wheat from the chaff" — and to discover that Jesus Christ *is* the center of *all* I am, *all* I believe.

Not that Christ had been left out — He hadn't. But I, however unintentionally, had by conformity and identity with fellow-missionaries failed to identify with my Lord.

Our vacation months were spent at the lovely seashore resort of Pei-tai-ho where missionaries of all denominations gathered and where summer conferences were held. At these conferences I viewed with suspicion any ideas coming from unfamiliar sources. Most of my interpretations of God's ways needed the approval of like-minded people from my own mission. So, when the subjects of "listening to God" and "definite guidance" came up, I dismissed them as matters about which I already knew.

However, when the subject of "absolute honesty" in confession arose, I protected myself by taking refuge in the fact that our mission did not go along with such teaching. Except of course for the unconverted! Certainly "confession" was not for the converted dedicated missionaries!

I had failed to take into consideration God and His abiding love and concern for all people, converted or unconverted! God, however, considered me. Just how, and to what extent He spoke to me, cannot here be fully told. But speak He did, even though I was an unwilling listener, who for almost three years had "heard" nothing.

I'm the kind who **must** always learn the hard way.

And before I learn I hit bottom every time. I now know God's love takes in the "whole picture" — the very essence and core of my total self — and if in the process of listening to Him it is necessary for me to get hurt, it will be a good hurting.

Looking back, I know God was speaking through all that happened: the emergency operation, the serious relapse, the week I hovered between life and death, the three months' convalescence. Flat on my back, I finally said, "All right, Lord, I'll listen. What is it this time?"

The answer was clear — unmistakable. It meant that once again the course of my life was to be changed.

Up to this time I'd been a secretary in the mission office, and not a very satisfied one, either. I longed to work with people — not paper work! Unsuccessfully, I'd tried to "surrender" this desire, and settle down to giving my very best to the work God had, for the time, given me to do.

Now, it was as though the Lord Jesus were saying, "You've been in office work long enough. This period of learning is over. Follow Me — into the villages of China — where the people sit in darkness and long for light."

My first objection was "But Lord, they'll kill me." (This was shortly after John and Betty Stam had been killed.) There were other objections: "There's no hot water, no running water, no bathrooms — it's so dirty out there in the villages." With God listening, my words and thought for my own comfort made me ashamed.

Then, it seemed as though the Lord Jesus said, "Rosalind, I understand. I came to earth because I was sent. It wasn't exactly what I had been used to either . . . and I was killed. Trust Me now. Take up your cross, My child, and follow Me. I was with you when you came here, and I'll be with you there, for I will never leave you."

I did as He asked, and He was with me.

In circumstances which forced me to listen, God had once again demonstrated His communicating love. Though I was an unwilling listener, God waited. The three months I lay flat on my back gave me plenty of time to think and to reflect, to finally recognize and to accept the love of God coming through to me. Love never forces. Nor does love reveal everything all at once. A step at a time God led me, but never faster than I was able to take each step. And always it was His loving encouragement which drew me on.

How does one become willing?

Not long ago a friend said, "Ros, I need the very material you are working on right now. Need it badly. But my problem is that although I know I need a miracle in my life, I'm not willing to accept changes in my life. How do I get willing?"

How do you become willing? Count on God's love. Believe He really is present and is attempting to communicate with you.

Cooperate with God. Tell Him you are willing to be made willing.

Make an all-out basic commitment to Jesus Christ — a commitment covering everything you know and believe, and everything you don't know but need to learn.

Trust God's great love for you. Know that He will never take unfair advantage. Admit He needs both your consent and cooperation.

Remind yourself that growth of any sort implies change, and that life is never static. Change must come and is essential not only for your own good but for your development and your progress.

Your mental attitude is half the battle. And you can learn to control your own conscious thoughts.

During the early years I experienced God's guidance, I thought He spoke only when there was something very important at hand. In a vital sense this is true, for *where* we are and *what* we are doing is important to God, who has an over-all plan that fits together. In another sense, each one of us is more important to God as a person than any work we may do for Him. Only when God has our attention, can we also give Him our cooperation.

Here let me emphasize the importance of response in continued communication if it is to be effective. We must not only be willing to be understood, but also to understand. Communication is a two-way street. The more I understand myself, the more you understand me, and the more you understand me, the more you'll understand yourself. In communication with God, we must let Him know we are willing to listen and ready to respond.

God is speaking all the time

On two occasions in the last few years, I have shared a convention platform with one of God's great men, Dr. Frank Laubach, author of many books, as well as the founder of the World Literacy Movement, Each One Teach One. He makes this statement which I'll never forget:

"God is speaking all the time, all the time, all the time."

When I first heard it, I thought about it all day.

If God is speaking all the time, what am I doing all that time?

Through Dr. Frank, modern miracles of faith have taken place. Illiterate peoples all over the world are learning to read, because one man learned to listen to God and to follow through.

I want to be listening all the time, all the time, all the time. I'm really no longer afraid, but I'm willing to listen because I'm absolutely convinced of God's great, never-changing, unconditional love for me, through Jesus Christ.

The little things, the day-by-day things, our comings and goings, our hurts and our disappointments, our friends and loved ones, little children, flowers, trees, what we read, how we spend our money, what we do with our leisure time — through everything God has something to say to us.

Since He's speaking all the time, all the time, all the time, I want to be listening all the time, don't you?

Love and fear do not go together.

"Perfect love casts out fear, for fear has torment."

God *is* love (not — God has love).

When He gives me Himself, He is giving me Love.

All I have, He has given to me.

When He is with me, within me, I am loved.

Here is the whole answer to unwillingness.

$\sim$

Review and study questions

1. Why aren't we willing to hear God speak to us? Find as many reasons as possible.

2. What are some of the ways by which God changes

our desires so that we are willing? Show how these ways really are part of His love.

3. Discuss: Love is vulnerable.

⌣

Meditation No. 3

Read: Acts 9:1-22
Subject: God's Patience.

1. God will not ask of me more than I am able to bear. He knows where I am, and will lead me a step at a time. He will not tell me more than I am able to hear. He is never in a hurry, and I don't need to be, either.

2. This is a good time to face that subject you may have been putting off. In what area is God trying to get your attention? Are you in the work He wants for you? Are you in the place He wants you to be? Fear or rebellion or unwillingness are good indications that there is inner confusion and conflict.

3. Take the first step. Write down what seems to be coming through. If in doubt, don't. Wait. Watch. See how, in love, God begins to prepare you. In His good time the right door will open. Trust Him.

⌣

~6~

We could be healed . . .
through prayer

Two kinds of people will be reading this chapter — the sick and the well. The in-between class, those who "just have something the matter," are included among the sick.

We think of health or the lack of illness as being ideal. However, a lack of disease does not necessarily imply health. People can be weary, disturbed, depressed or discouraged, and still not have anything physically wrong with them. Physical illness is one thing, but the illness of the spirit is another. Sometimes these affect each other, more than we are willing to admit, more than we can ever imagine. The heart or spirit of man can be as sick as the body, and can need healing even more.

Recently I was reading an article in the *Chicago Tribune* on foster homes. I was interested to learn why hospitals have discontinued their wards for unwanted babies. Even babies know the difference between being loved and not being loved, and react accordingly. They become listless, stop moving around, lie on their backs all day, fail to show interest or response, and eventually fail to develop the strong bodies God intends them to have when they aren't given love. The doctors can order

T.L.C. (tender loving care) on the chart, but who in a busy hospital has time to give it to them?

Adults can be classified in the same way: those who are loved and those who are not. In which classification are you? Love is such a personal matter. It is a person-to-person relationship. If you are remembering *when* you were loved or wishing you were loved, this chapter is for you. If you are one of the loved-right-now persons, this chapter is for you, too.

There is nothing like a new love affair to make a woman beautiful — a woman of any age! She blossoms! Her skin, her eyes, her hair, her voice, everything about her becomes filled with new vitality. Life itself takes on new meaning with the new love. A conversion experience or a fresh awareness of God's love can produce the same results.

Being loved is a matter of the heart, and so is prayer. Prayer is the language of the heart. Both involve giving-receiving relationships. Deny the heart either of these expressions, and it can soon become like a parched, neglected garden — no flowers, only dry dead memories — and desperately in need of spiritual healing.

Spiritual healing

I first heard the words "spiritual healing" through the Order of Saint Luke, Episcopal in origin but now inter-denominational. I remember saying the words over and over — *spiritual healing.* I thought about them. I liked them. When the spirit is sick . . . how is it healed? When the spirit is well . . . how does it get sick? Is one healing enough? Physically we need healing many times, and I am convinced the same is true of spiritual healing.

Spiritual healing is the healing of the soul (the spirit)

when by faith in God, through Jesus Christ our Lord, we receive the forgiveness of our sins.

I've given much thought to the many fundamental Christians whose one and only spiritual healing took place at the time of their conversion. None has occurred since their acceptance of Christ as their personal Saviour.

After conversion, where does spiritual healing come in? As Protestants, we confess our sins privately to God — when or where is our own business. Whether we do it at all is also our own business. That we seldom do is witnessed by our friends who also witness our afflictions, our illnesses, our attitudes not only toward ourselves but toward life in general.

Confession of sin can be compared to eating three balanced meals. If meals are prepared for us and we have a regular place to eat, we prosper; if not we suffer accordingly. By the same token, when there is a time and place for facing ourselves, our failures, our sins against God and others, and we learn to confess — we grow. If not, we suffer spiritual malnutrition and its attendant negative results.

Physical healing

An astute young psychiatrist recently told me it had been his original intention to specialize in internal medicine until it was brought to his attention that more than half the patients whom doctors treat are suffering from psychosomatic illnesses.

The importance of this subject has prompted me in recent months to speak at least once on the subject of mentally-induced illness while conducting workshops on prayer. Not that anyone deliberately chooses to be ill! But all unknowingly the mind has incredible powers to dismiss and to suppress the unacceptable. The suscepti-bility of the body which must bear the brunt of this mental dismissal is likewise almost unbelievable.

Leslie Weatherhead's 500-page book *Psychology, Religion and Healing* (paper, $1.75; Abingdon, Apex D-6) lists some of the illnesses which could be spiritual in origin: gastric and duodenal ulcers, some forms of skin irritations, allergies, asthma, spastic colon and paralysis. These illnesses may indicate not only disharmony be-tween the mind and circumstances but also between the soul and God.

Another book which will stimulate your faith is by the late Dr. Edgar Sanford, *God's Healing Power* (Pren-tice-Hall, 1959). This is excellent reading and is filled with stories of real people.

To be healed spiritually or physically means that one is the recipient of God's power. "Ask and ye shall re-ceive," said Jesus. Is that all one has to do to be healed? ". . . pray one for another, that ye may be healed," wrote James (5:16). Have someone pray for me? Learn to pray myself? Why don't people practice these two means of healing if they work?

If we could read each other's minds, it might help us to locate our tension points. But we can't. And half the time we can't accurately interpret our own thoughts, let alone make up our own minds. We know something is wrong, but cannot find the cause. Or, we can't face the real source of the trouble, so in order to bear the pain, we use our minds to rationalize the problem.

In my own life, I have many times unwittingly re-pressed unpleasant things. The antidote or opposite would have been to recognize and face them. Mentally pushing problems away only results in having them come to the surface again as physical ailments. I suffered severe gall-bladder attacks and was almost ready for major surgery when I discovered my basic trouble was not physical in origin, but emotional. It was insecurity.

This followed my resignation from the Oriental Missionary Society (because China became Communist) and occurred before I learned what the next step in God's plan for me was to be. Hadn't I prayed? Yes, I had. Didn't I believe God would show me? Yes, I did. Wasn't I trusting Him and His love? Yes, I was — that is, consciously, verbally I was. The proof that this was not sufficient became quite evident — severe and painful gall-bladder attacks.

Unconsciously, my mind had played a trick on me. My thoughts were in a turmoil of confusion and insecurity concerning the future and soon became physically manifest in a very real and painful way. I can't recall any specific dynamic healing, but I can recall reaffirming my belief in God's love and plan for me. And I can recall having friends lay hands on me to pray for my recovery. I did recover and have never since had another attack.

Later, I suffered from gastric disorders which eventually developed into a duodenal ulcer. I knew what was wrong, initially, but the symptoms continued for seven years after the cause disappeared. The cause was psychosomatic and mentally induced, but the pain persisted, and X-rays revealed scar tissue. Perhaps all ulcer patients are not psychosomatic casualties. I found it somewhat comforting to learn that many ulcer patients are high-salaried or creative people with many responsibilities!

In the course of my travels, I sometimes had a pre-scription from a new doctor. On one occasion, hoping to receive advice, I told the doctor what I believed was the origin of my trouble. He was not only embarrassed but changed the subject. I then realized why so many people needlessly suffer.

Why didn't this doctor help me? Because his practice dealt only with things physical. Should the healing of spiritual illnesses be out of an M.D.'s line simply because he is not a clergyman?

This is where I believe we who call ourselves Christian are wrong. No matter what the need, as creative persons in whom God's Spirit lives we are all committed to one another, as the branches are to each other and to the vine. We are committed to help one another, pray for one another, love one another. No man lives unto himself alone. When one man finds his way, many find their way; when one man loses his way, many lose their way.

The Menninger Foundation in Topeka, Kansas, has com-bined all aspects of human illness — physical, spiritual and mental — in order to treat the entire man. More and more of this type of treatment is available, but church acceptance lags far behind. Congratulations to all who are moving in this direction!

My ulcers? Yes, they are gone! How did they go? When I prayed and confessed my failures, needs, and sins — both alone and with a trusted friend. I tried honestly to eliminate contributing causes. In prayer I listen for God's voice and try to live one day at a time. Since entering this present phase of my life — writing books, lecturing, and holding Prayer Workshops — I have been well. I have accepted God's love for me, and I have accepted myself as I am.

My own experiences have alerted me to the suffering of others. Recently a friend told me how faith and prayer ended his asthma attacks, which were especially frequent during high school days. After he went to college he learned that asthma is often a psychosomatic illness generated by unrecognized guilt feelings or unsatisfactory relationships. Seeking God's help in prayer, he faced up and finally found the root of his trouble: his mother.

"I was completely freed from all symptoms of asthma," said D.S., "when I was able to forgive my mother, and to love her with the new love with which God strengthened me. I've been set free — from resentment and asthma."

In a certain city, a lady who was driving me to an appointment told me about her sister's three-year-old child, who suffered from asthma. I asked the question, "How do her parents get along?"

After several blocks of silence, the answer came. "Well, the wife wears the pants in the family."

I then learned there is also an eight-year-old son who suffers from skin allergies! Who could guess that subtle pressures, often unspoken between husband and wife, could affect two innocent children? Nor what would happen — if parents learned to listen to God and pray together? Afraid? Possibly at first, because of the changes honesty might bring, but not when some caring friend assures them of God's waiting love.

To be spiritually healed we must be in the healing presence of the great God who loves us. Being in His Presence means accepting what He wants to give us.

Acceptance in all areas: the trouble, the estrangement, the silence, the denial, the delay, the resentment, the other person, one's self. Acceptance of God's love for me, just as I am. Acceptance of the other person, just as he is. Most of all, acceptance of God's forgiveness, for what I have done and for the way I am.

Fresh, sweet, total forgiveness! Forgiveness is the most healing therapy in the world. To be forgiven by God, by our fellowmen, and to forgive ourselves — this is healing and this is wholeness. Can you remember when it happened to you? It should happen again. It can. It might cost you your private opinion, giving up your favorite "story," or your treasured resentment. But it just might be that in so doing, you will find healing and the blessing of release.

⌐

For reflection and thought

1. One friend, after reading my manuscript, wrote at the close of the last paragraph of this chapter: What about Amy Carmichael? Yes, sometimes God's saints are not healed. They are confined, and in the midst of suffering prove God's grace to be sufficient. Amy Carmichael was a great missionary to India's children, whose later years were spent in bed because of a bone that refused to heal. Her room became a literal shrine of healing to all others who stepped within.

2. Forgiveness. There is so much more that needs to be said on this subject. More will be written in chapters 14 and 15.

⌐

⁓ 7 ⁓

We could pray . . . if only we'd be children

Children are so unself-conscious.

I remember a three-year-old Chinese child all dressed up for Sunday school. Pleased with herself and eager to show me a new item of clothing, she reached to her ankles for the hem of her *cheong-sham* (long outer garment) and with one swift movement lifted her skirts up over her face — exposing her short panties and her bare midriff! All this to show me her new stockings! But more important, to share with me her great delight and joy.

Children have no self-consciousness. Adults are plagued with it. This is one of the reasons why adults find communication difficult. Oh, to be a little child in God's presence!

When Jesus answered the question, "Who is the greatest in the kingdom of Heaven?" He called a child, set him in front of them, and said, "I tell you this: unless you turn round and become like children, you will never enter the kingdom of Heaven. Let a man humble himself till he is like this child, and he will be the greatest in the kingdom of Heaven" (Matthew 18:1-4, NEB).

We are self-conscious because we are not childlike.

We are self-conscious because we are aware of others and their reactions to us, chiefly their approval or disapproval. So the rat-race of self-deception and mask-wearing goes on!

We aim at perfection but are easily discouraged. One friend told me that after she's prayed aloud in the presence of others, her mind would be full of questions: "Did I do it right? I wonder if I said the right things? What did Mrs. So-and-so think of me? What a fool I made of myself!"

Unable to recognize the "voices" within her, she could not tell whether she was talking to herself, or whether "another" was using her inner self to project failure so that next time she wouldn't even try. The false motive of "approval by others" can cloud the issue with confusions. I've learned that when I turn my thoughts to Jesus Christ (who alone knows my motives) I am able to reject false ideas and hold steady.

Prayer is when you talk to Jesus, said a child, when asked for a definition. Prayer is also when you think of Jesus. For some adults prayer is more difficult than making a speech in public.

In a little town in Wisconsin I held a prayer workshop for women of a Classis of the Reformed Church. The pastor's wife told me of an elderly lady who had longed to pray, but so far had been unable to do so. Each week before she came to prayer meeting, she would carefully write out her prayer, memorize it and put it in her purse. During the prayer-time, with trembling fingers cold as ice, she would unfold the little slip of paper — which she already knew by heart. Try as she might, she was unable to lift her voice to even read what she had so carefully prepared. Furthermore, so preoccupied was she with this effort that she scarcely heard the prayers of others. Each time she went home, she secretly hoped that the next time she might be able to participate.

I also recall an older woman in a New England town who found the love of the group gave her courage to start to pray audibly. The next morning she came back relaxed and smiling. "I slept last night without sleeping pills for the first time in five years! More than that, when my favorite granddaughter called this morning from college, (as she usually does) she said, 'Grandma, what's happened to you?' When I asked what she meant, she replied, 'You sound so relaxed, your voice sounds soft and different!' "

If you are agreeing with what I've written, why not ask God to help you be creative enough to find His way to set up a prayer service in your church? Ask His guidance that even the most fearful will want to participate and thus begin to find freedom. Why should any prayer meeting result in people carrying away more self-condemnation than they brought with them?

If prayer is talking to Jesus, why not stop *trying to pray,* and just talk to Him? Why should anyone condemn themselves for the way in which they do or do not pray? Whose approval do we want? There is no special way to pray that wins God's approval. He loves us no matter what we do, or how we pray.

Children are not self-conscious

We could learn to pray, if only we'd be as little children — unself-conscious. Children don't think beforehand what they will say to Jesus. They just say it. Whatever comes to their minds, whatever is in their hearts — they say it. They do this instinctively because they are aware of His love, and feel no need to protect themselves.

Self-conscious protection is the farthest idea from their little minds.

Children do not think in theological terms of God, but rather in the love-terms of the heart. They have an inner sense about people and know when they are liked or disliked. I'm not suggesting that we ignore our minds, and throw out our theology, but we do suffer from "adult-itis" — the lack of being loved. We lack the simplicity to follow our hearts into the presence of Jesus who is always ready to make known His love for us.

Childlikeness is a state of mind within us. When my mother was 83 she made this remark: "I sometimes can't believe this old body is mine. One thing I know, it is not *me*. The real me is still like the little girl who ran around my father's farm in Minnesota." My mother's active mind had a mental picture of herself which gave her an openness and a teachableness which kept her young in spirit.

By contrast there was the friend who drove me to several cities in the East. He had a "block" in his mind because of a mental picture of himself, but I don't think he was aware of it. He was an older man of considerable weight but not much height. On one occasion as he wedged himself behind the wheel, he laughed and said, "Funny thing, I know I ought to take off some weight, but in my own mind I am still a slim young man in my 20's!"

In plain English, one of these was childlike because of an open mind, while the other was childish because of a closed mind.

The power of imagination

This is another quality which children possess which

I'm learning to develop, mainly because it makes God more real. There is no problem about praying or prayer when God is real. Children have no difficulty in believing Jesus is right there with them. To them all of life is a fairy story. Imagination is a gift we should help them cherish and channel.

One evening last year a child forced me into an imaginary situation which taught me a great deal about the release and freedom which can accompany imagination. I had not seen Paul and Marie Little since their marriage, so it was with real pleasure that I accepted their invitation to dinner. I sat in the living room while Marie got dinner and Paul and little son were in the garage. The five-year-old daughter came into the room but paid no attention to me, although we had been introduced upon my arrival.

Thinking to make friends, I said encouragingly, "Hi, how are you?"

She continued to ignore me completely. Rather shyly, as if she were alone, she went from one chair to another, touching and patting one arm after another, all the while avoiding my eyes as if I weren't there. I waited, delighted at the quiet opportunity to watch such a charming child. She went to the window, lifted the curtain lightly, looked out a moment, put it down, stood there another moment, and then suddenly without a trace of shyness walked over, sat down beside me and spoke.

"What's your 'maginary name?"

I rose to the occasion and said the first thing that popped into my mind. "My 'maginary name is Margery. What's yours?"

"Mine's Barbara."

She then settled back against the cushions quite secure in her 'maginary role. As two imaginary people we had real conversation. No strangeness, no shyness, but freedom to talk, to laugh, and to make up anything we wanted to say. She was a different little girl because she could get outside of herself in her role as Barbara, and she could accept me as a friend she knew, not a total stranger.

If we could but transfer the idea inherent in this story to the practice of prayer, and imagine ourselves little children in the presence of Jesus (who loves little children) prayer would be more relaxed and natural than even talking with each other.

For children, the power of imagination carries over into religion, as it also should for adults. I want to say more about this subject of "imagination in prayer" in a later chapter, when we talk about God's presence with us, to show how God wants our minds as well as our hearts. In fact, He needs our minds and our imaginations to make Himself real to us. He created our minds in the first place in order to communicate with us.

One reason it is difficult for adults to pray is because our Father seems so far away — away up in heaven somewhere! The "Person" we are addressing is not present, or so it would seem, if we would listen to the tone of our voices and the content of our words.

Pray with your children

Did you ever stop to think how children pray? And to whom they pray? Whom does your child address when he prays? "Dear Jesus . . ." Have you ever considered why children pray to Jesus, while their parents pray, "Our Father"?

I'll tell you why. Because Jesus is real to children.

They come home from Sunday school with pictures of
Jesus blessing the children, Jesus healing the sick, Jesus
teaching and feeding the crowd. They sing about Him:
"Jesus loves me this I know." "Jesus loves the little child-
dren of the world."

Listen to them pray and you'll know Jesus is real to
them. They tell Him everything and no subject is considered out-of-bounds until they begin to imitate the
prayers of their elders. Then too often they begin to
lose interest in church and religion altogether.

Recently as a guest in the Glenn Torrey home in Kansas, I was invited to teach the family conversational
prayer. We had just finished supper.

"Shall we pull up that chair for Jesus?" I suggested to
the five-year old. Sliding off her chair, she pulled the
empty one from the wall to a place beside her own.
Then sitting down, she looked dubiously at the chair
and then at me.

"Will Jesus sit in a high-chair?" she asked.

"Why don't you ask Him?" I replied.

Looking at the chair a moment while we waited, she
began to nod her head, "Yes, He says He will."

Prayer begins with the presence of Jesus with us,
"whom having not seen, we love."

Perhaps you could begin to pray by praying with
children — yours, or someone else's. I remember a father
I met in Bermuda who told me it was impossible for
him to pray when others were present because he didn't
have the right language. (He meant the King-James-
Shakespearian language.) Then he amended his statement.

"Well, I do pray with my two boys. They're eight
and ten. When I pray with them, I'm one of them. That's

the best time of the day for me, because I can talk to Jesus right from my heart like the boys do."

I couldn't resist asking, "What do you think might happen between your wife and yourself, if you two could communicate through prayer-dialogue like that?"

He threw up his hands and shook his head. "Impossible! Neither of us could be like children with each other!"

Impossible? What is not possible with man *is* possible with God. In His loving presence it is not necessary to wear a mask for protection, for prayer is an open highway for the expression of love from His heart to ours.

⌐

> They brought children for him to touch; and the disciples scolded them for it. But when Jesus saw this, he was indignant, and said to them, 'Let the children come to me; do not try to stop them; for the kingdom of God belongs to such as these. . . .' And he put his arms around them, laid his hands upon them, and blessed them.
>
> Mark 10:13-16, NEB.

⌐

When love is present, the message is heard.

⌐

~8~

Even if we doubt . . . we can pray

Summary: Chapters 1-7.

Our first lessons in learning to communicate have stressed the importance of listening to and recognizing the various voices within us, and the necessity of admitting our own need for spiritual or physical healing, for love, for acceptance, for being what God wants us to be and where He has planned for us to be.

Then there is the need to be childlike, to be willing to have old patterns broken, fears healed, and forgiveness become reality. We need the childlike attitude of simplicity and honesty which rests completely in the loving intentions of our Father. As we begin to speak to Him from our hearts, we experience His blessing of healing upon us.

Perhaps you long to do this, but feel like such a hypocrite — trying to believe God loves you when you know perfectly well you don't even love yourself, let alone anyone else. So how can God — who apparently knows everything about everybody — love you?

Faith and doubt coexist to some degree within everyone, both for those who profess some belief in Christianity, and for those who do not.

The conversation in the jet plane (chapter 3)

prompted me to think deeply about many things I'd simply taken for granted. I began to realize that facing
doubt and uncertainty, especially with regard to what
one believes about God, is a part of life, just as life is a
part of prayer.

Those insinuating questions about God's intentions toward me, and the whole human race, were not easy to
forget. In fact, I haven't forgotten them, for at the time,
and for the first time in my life, I was experiencing doubt
about God's love for me. As a teen-ager I'd never been
plagued with so-called doubts. Now, however, I found
myself unable to forget the ideas presented to me on
that plane trip.

Later I repeated some of these "questions" to my
friend, Eugenia Price. I'll never forget her answer: "If
you'd lived a great portion of your life as an agnostic as
I have, you'd know what it's really like to live without
God. I never want to go through those years again. I
know there's a God and I know He loves me!"

Also I remember a statement made by Bill Starr, direc-
tor of Young Life Campaign. "You haven't begun to
know what you believe until you have had a few doubts."

What fallacy in our thinking makes us tell young
people not to doubt, when facing doubts is often the beginning of maturity?

As for myself, after the experience related, I learned
more about the truth of God's love than I ever before
knew. And, increasingly I realize how much more there
is to learn! There was a time when people with serious
doubts and questions about God disturbed me; now I
can smile with understanding while assuring them they
are on the road to new discoveries.

Questions which today seem to disturb many religious

people are: Does one have to be a Christian to pray? Can God hear the prayer of an unconverted person? Doesn't the Bible say God hears only one prayer from the sinner — "Be merciful to me a sinner"?

These questions became the focal point of very strong emotional reactions among the more than 700 women attending a weekend conference near Detroit, where I appeared as one of the speakers.

In chapter 2 I have written of my own discovery concerning how very much our Father God loves people. As for "sinners," their path is already obstructed by stumbling blocks of doubt. They can't believe in God's love for them, nor in God's willingness to hear them. If those bearing the name "Christian" also insist that God refuses to hear people until they have been converted — how can any person ever be encouraged to approach God? Each must be assured that God's love reaches out to him personally, that any sincere prayer initiated in his heart will be heard by God.

At the conference mentioned, I began to understand in a very clear way why more non-Christian people do not feel "worthy" to approach God in prayer. It may, in part, be attributed to the dogmatism and bigotry of Christian people having no real message of love to give, and no real love in their hearts for the person still outside the doors of the church.

Does it disturb you to think that God might be bigger than you think He is? That He might be the kind of God who would hear the prayer of an unconverted man or woman?

This concept did deeply disturb many of the women, and one woman in particular, who came to speak with me personally. Realizing her questions could not be resolved in a ten-minute conversation, I suggested, "My dear, go back to your room and talk with your Lord about this. What I say or don't say has nothing to do with what you believe. Truth, however, can at times be very painful, especially when love and theology appear to contradict one another." (I was remembering some of the things which had earlier disturbed me before I discovered what the Bible really says.) "Take time," I continued, "to read and to think. God will reveal to you the truth."

Sometimes we speak the truth dogmatically, as if there were no possible relationship between "what I believe" and "what you believe." Despite every indication to the contrary, separately held truths need not invalidate one another. Such lack of understanding may not only block our own thinking but hinder those hesitant to approach Jesus Christ.

However, whether we unintentionally (dogmatically) block our thinking or unintentionally (unlovingly) hinder others, there is an all-wise, all-loving God who has already completed His plan and His purpose in history. There will be nothing that can hinder His love from eventually coming through to you and to me.

When I think of the varying beliefs I have held in my lifetime, and remember that my Father God loved me through each phase with an everlasting love — I am at His feet in heart-worship. What a great God! The slowness and blindness and obstinacy of religious dogma does not hinder a loving God from loving those who hold such tenets.

The initiative of God, the eternal planning of God, the loving kindness of God shown to us through Christ — these tell us that He is willing to wait for every one of us.

Our learning process is slow. It is painful to change an opinion. But God waits, because He knows what He has done for us.

I've been reading the first chapter of Ephesians in the Paraphrased Epistles, *Living Letters,* by Kenneth N. Taylor, (Tyndale House, Wheaton, Ill., 1962), and it is as though I had never read it before — so fresh and clear is the truth regarding the riches of God's concern and care and love for us.

> Long ago before He made the world God chose us to be His very own, through what Christ would do for us; He decided then to make us holy in His eyes, without a single fault — we who stand before Him covered with His love. His unchanging plan has always been to adopt us into His own family by sending Jesus Christ to die for us. And He did this because He wanted to! Now all praise to God for His wonderful kindness to us and His favor that He has poured out upon us, because we belong to His dearly loved Son. So overflowing is His kindness towards us that He took away all our sins through the blood of His Son, by Whom we are saved; And He has showered down upon us the richness of His grace — for how well He understands us and knows what is best for us at all times.
>
> Ephesians 1:4-8

True or false?

Mark them for yourself, and give your reasons. Many persons take the opposite view from you. Could you tell them, or convince them of your viewpoint? Could you see their viewpoint? What about God's viewpoint?

_____One has to be a Christian in order to pray.

_____The only prayer God hears from a sinner is, "God, be merciful to me, a sinner."

_____God loves the converted more than the sinner.

_____God couldn't possibly love me as I am.

_____God is for me, not against me.

_____God loves me, even if I don't love myself.

⁓9⁓

We can pray . . . despite intellectual doubts

Recently I talked with a young man, who, because of his views about evolution, etc., thought he couldn't become a Christian. This potential believer had obviously been misinformed by well-intentioned Christians. The Bible clearly tells us that all we have to do to be "saved" is to believe on the Lord Jesus Christ (Acts 16: 30, 31).

Were these Christians introducing this young man to a set of theological tenets with intellectual proof, or were they introducing him to a Person who loves him? If to a Person, why not start with an introduction, make communication possible, and let them speak together?

"But what about repentance, forgiveness, the cross, and all the things you should have told him?" cries the eager, longing-to-be-right person.

Haven't you seen it happen? I have.

The moment that young man and I stopped talking *about* Christ and began to speak *to Him,* faith asserted itself. The gift was given, the miracle took place. He belonged. Assurance was given in that very moment. Does anyone ever become a meaningful person to us until we meet and speak with them by name?

Later that same evening and all the next day, this young man recalled many things he'd heard about the

Christian faith. He began to fit together truths which had appeared to contradict one another. His excitement over these discoveries was contagious. Now he was being taught by the Spirit of God.

Did anyone ever get a degree in Science by standing outside the science buildings and waiting for someone to convince him of the secret of the atom?

Is our God not great enough to reach a man just where he is? Is He limited by a certain pattern, a certain approach, a certain theology? Can we not trust Him to open whatever door is necessary for a searching heart to enter?

If we want to know we are loved by God, we should try to meet people who love Him. We would want them to give us an introduction and we would want to speak directly to Christ. We would want to be like little children coming home, coming in out of the long dark night. Certainly we would want someone to take us by the hand and welcome us.

We will do well to remember that all doubt is not intellectual, even though it may seem to be. There are usually some unseen emotional factors as we discovered in Chapter 8.

A college student writes

> Dear Ros: What about the doubts *after* I'm a Christian? Can I still be a child of God and yet question the validity of the Christian faith? I think I believe . . . I acknowledge the love and existence of Christ, but I don't seem to feel it anymore. K.

My letter to her

> Dear K: It is not wrong to doubt. Doubt does not necessarily destroy faith. In the end it can strengthen your faith.

Faith and doubt can coexist. You must not be afraid to question, and don't be too proud to ask. God's truth does not have to be defended. Trust is not based on 'feeling' but on Christ Himself.

You are coming into a maturity of your own where you must think these things through for yourself. Only then will you have a faith which is yours, not that of your parents or others.

Sometimes a mental picture helps us. Think of your left hand representing all your doubts and questions, your right hand, belief and trust in God. Shall you then cut off your left hand because it doesn't serve the same purpose as your right hand? With the loss of one, you hinder the other. Likewise, shall we cut off faith because doubt is present? It is equally unsatisfactory to submerge doubt in an effort to make faith continue.

"Lord, I believe, help thou mine unbelief," cried the father with his sick son there before Jesus Himself. He was heard, and received more than he asked, for our Lord is always a generous Giver.

Again, picture a chemical solution.

I sometimes hold my questions "in solution," (of faith) because I refuse to let that which I do not understand undermine that which I know. If I wait, my uncertainties will begin to crystalize, one by one, and sooner or later, I'll know and understand the truth.

C. S. Lewis did this. No doubt you've read some of his books? As a young man he repudiated his faith but later it all came back to him. His books are of two kinds: (1) those which proceed on a water-tight logical basis about things we need to believe — amazingly clear and simple — such as, *Mere Christianity;* (2) those which deal with ideas and truths which cannot be reasoned out by human logic, but which are nevertheless true, such as his novel *Perelandra.*

Jesus Christ appeals again and again to the love-need in our hearts, seldom to the reason and logic of our minds. There are many good books on the validity of the Old and New Testament documents you should read for your own information, but it is well to remember that the power of love is greater than the power of reason.

I'd like to close this letter on a more personal note, and tell you that in my brief acquaintance with you, I admire you for your independent, honest thinking. Take your time now, don't feel pushed. My prayers are with you. Remember, God loves you. Jesus loves you. And so do I.   —*Ros.*

P.S. (after receiving an answer to the above letter).

One sentence in that letter was more prophetic than I knew. "It is well to remember that the power of love is greater than the power of reason." I discovered through later correspondence, that one of the reasons for this deep disturbance was a growing relationship with a young man of Jewish background, and her inability to quickly bring some loose ends of her thinking together.

Counselors to young people soon learn to look for some deeper underlying emotional problem which triggers the more obvious, the intellectual one. Since we are susceptible to emotional situations, let us take time to work things out, for God has given us both emotion and intellect to act as a balance and counter-balance.

Pray to the Saviour who knows your thoughts before you utter them, and your own thinking will begin to clear.

Count on Christ being there, whether you feel like it or not. He is there. He remains constant no matter how you fluctuate.

Read chapter 7 again, and come to Him as a little child. Speak directly to Jesus Christ — call Him by Name. Cast yourself before Him — and then having done all this, go on with the business of living. He'll come through just at the right time. Something will catch your attention and give you "the message" just when you are ready — a book, a person, an event, a word, a song. Ideas will crystalize.

You have a lifetime to discover the answers to your questions. Growth and maturity come through asking questions. Creativity comes through alertness. Honesty is a vital part of growth, of having faith.

Sometimes it's more fun to find out what home is like from the inside then from the outside.

Home is a place where love is more important than unanswered questions.

Home is a place where one can learn through failure because there is love with caring, acceptance and communication.

Home is a place where there is a person who loves you.

Home is being with the Lord Jesus.

⌐

Some more questions

1. Read the true or false statements which follow. Mark them.
2. What kind of a doubter are you?
   a. Are you an honest doubter? Some people prefer to doubt, so they will never have to accept an answer, or make a decision.
   b. Do your doubts stretch your mind and take you beyond yourself? Or do they merely make you confused and critical?

⌐

True or false?

Read, mark, and give your reasons for or against in each case.

----------Faith and doubt can exist together.

----------One is stronger in his beliefs after he has questioned them.

----------If I have any doubts, I can't be a believer.

----------A man can become a Christian even if he does believe in evolution.

----------A man can be a Christian and believe in evolution.

----------I can be a child of God and still have questions about the validity of the Christian faith.

----------There has to be *more* than we know about God.

----------God has to be greater than ideas any mind or any book can contain.

----------Facing one's doubts honestly is the beginning of maturity.

----------One does not know what he really believes until he has had a few doubts and questions.

Part III. New Attitudes about Prayer

~10~

God's kind of love

That we do not love one another, or even ourselves, is the major tragedy of the human race. Contradictory as it may seem, deep within us we want love more than anything in the world; yet divorce rates increase, lonely people continue to live alone, and within the average family hearts break for lack of knowing how to give true expressions of love.

> Ever since I can remember [writes L.K.], I've wanted my mother to put her arms around me and love me. But when I got within hearing distance of her, she'd be complaining or ill — she was very dramatic at either. Anyway, I never received the love I longed for, so consoled myself by thinking any show of affection was "puppy love" yet all the time starving for real love. The resentment within me began to express itself in withdrawal, the very opposite of what I wanted.
>
> I grew up with the image of receiving the deep true love of a good man. When I married I knew it was a mistake, and it was. We're divorced. Now here I am at 47, with that same deep longing within (like a rat gnawing away on wood) for a good husband, companion, friend or loved one. It isn't that I haven't met attractive men, but I can't seem to show how I feel. All my life I have pretended and played a part.

Many might have written this same letter. Everywhere people long to be loved, to recapture lost love, or to find new love. The longing persists, despite the unfortunate but familiar spectres of jealousy, hurt feelings, indifference, estrangement, separation, or divorce. The search continues — always with the hope of finding the "one right person" who will satisfy the love-hunger within our hearts.

We look for love from our parents, we hope for it from our companions, we long for it from our spouses. We are past masters at demanding and possessing. Yet how limited we are in giving — especially in giving of ourselves and our love. Not knowing how to give love, we are unable to accept love, and how empty is the deepness of that inner well within us.

Jesus understood this quality of the human heart, this ever-present longing for love. He understood the lonely woman of Samaria whose search was leading her in the wrong direction. Five husbands had not satisfied the deep longing in her heart. To her, He said . . .

> Everyone who drinks this water [from the well] will be thirsty again, but whoever drinks the water I will give him will never be thirsty again. For my gift will become a spring in the man himself, welling up into eternal life.
>
> John 4:13, 14; Phillips

The well water of human love never quenches — one is always thirsty with a thirst never really satisfied. The water which Jesus gives promises to quench the thirst of the one who drinks, becoming within him an artesian well, springing up now and forever with God's love.

God *is* love and God *has* love.

Those who are beginners in receiving love grasp only at the latter; God has love. This implies that God's love is a gift, which indeed it is, given generously and unceasingly to us. But there is more, much more, for the one who gives to God an open mind and a receptive heart. There is the gift of knowing and understanding that God *is* love, of knowing God is within us, knowing Christ is within us, knowing, therefore, we have within us the Source of Love, the Power of Love. We only need to send "flash-thoughts" of recognition to make Love and Power available to us — for God is love.

"How does God's love operate?" asked a man at the close of a workshop. "Can the ashes of a dead love be revived?"

C. S. Lewis in his writings on love states that most human love fades to dry dust before those involved will give God an opportunity to come up with a new living shoot — which is God's kind of love.

"I still have a very poor understanding of the behavior and attitudes of Christians," wrote a woman who has suffered much at the hands of well-intentioned believers ` — suffered because she was a nonconformist.

As Christians we ought to be able to forgive and to love people despite the wrong, odd, strange, eccentric or stupid things they may do. That we are unable for the most part to do so is evident everywhere — not only in personal lives but in the serious situations facing our world today. Christian or non-Christian, black or white, we tend not to love those different from ourselves, or those who do not agree with us. We shut them out and go our own way.

There are aspects of human love we need to recognize before we can either talk about or understand God's love. These involve our ability or inability to give and receive love — to accept or reject love. They distinguish human love from God's love.

Reuel L. Howe, in his book *Herein Is Love* (Judson

Press, 1961, pp. 33-34), states the problem of human love very clearly.

> Human love can be ambiguous; we do not know whether it is safe to give and to accept love. It is a risk both to love and to accept love, and all of us to some degree are afraid to take the risk.
>
> Human fellowship is both heroic and tragic; it is both renewing and destructive; it is both healing and hurtful, but it is indispensable to life. This is our human predicament.
>
> Something is needed to cut into the ambiguity of human love. This is what Christ does. He draws the confused currents of human love into the unifying stream of Divine love, thus making possible a new relationship.

In his analysis of our inability to love one another Mr. Howe gives us four suggestions for drawing human love "into the unifying stream of Divine love."

1. That we accept "dying" to ourselves and our point of view as a part of living. Jesus said (Mark 8:35), "For whosoever will save his life shall lose it; but whosoever shall lose his life for my sake . . . the same shall save it." If we die to ourselves we will not be surprised nor shocked by the violations of ideal behavior in human relations.

2. That we face, accept, see through and behind the wrong things people do.

3. That because Christ on the cross accepted the unacceptable in all men, we are able to accept the unacceptable in ourselves.

4. That God's Spirit seeks to incarnate Himself in us today, in all our decisions, actions, and relationships. "Communication," states Mr. Howe, "is contained in the giving of oneself to another."

The question is, since communication seems to fail before it ever gets started, how are we going to carry out this Divine-love level of communication?

The key to communication

What is the real key to love and communication? How do we find it? Seldom do we receive lucid help or clear guide lines. During the past several years, I've read many books on communication. Nevertheless I still encounter situations where failure to communicate my real intent resulted in inadvertently hurting others.

I sincerely believe there is but one answer. The answer is prayer, the kind of prayer Jesus taught as recorded in Matthew 18:19, 20 (Phillips):

> If two of you on earth agree in asking for anything it will be granted to you by my Heavenly Father. For wherever two or three people come together in my name, I am there, right among them!

I believe, teach, and have seen demonstrated that Divine love is most effectively communicated through prayer, especially conversational prayer. Because dialogue praying involves all who are present, all should be, at any time, ready to participate. This creates an interest which makes such concentration a pleasure. The result is a spontaneous "agreeing as we ask" for things we had heretofore not even thought of, — an agreeing that makes possible the "granting" cited in the above Scripture.

In the traditional monologue prayer, one person often prays his way around the world while others present sit back and (well, what did *you* do?) wait for him to return!

Conversational prayer affords an opportunity to communicate with Divine love, because Jesus (who is the personification of this love) said, "wherever two or three people come together in my name, *I am there,* right among them!"

Conversational prayer permits an honest revealing of one's self without using clichés to mask our thoughts. It starts with surface needs, and proceeds to depth needs at the pace of those present. It is participating in one another's prayers at the very point of need, as Jesus would do in person, without introducing half a dozen irrelevant ideas. In the last three chapters we will examine in more detail how this may be done.

Only Divine love entering into and reinforcing human love will give us courage to open our hearts and to ask for what we need. Jesus encouraged us to ask and to receive. He knew that in the act of prayer our hearts are more receptive and our motives more clear, than at any other time.

Only in the presence of Jesus is it possible for Him to make known the love, the help, the joy, and the peace of mind and heart He intends for us. Without Him, we mistrust each other and doubt ourselves.

The 15th chapter of the gospel of John is a classic description of the life of believers together, living together, loving one another, asking and receiving with joy. There is a different atmosphere when together we acknowledge Jesus is right among us. And He is always among us — we need only to turn our minds to Him to experience His presence. There is no mask that can hide our face from Him or His face from us. All He requires of us is that we become as little children, trusting and being no longer afraid to assume the responsibilities of loving one another because we know we are loved.

How love operates

Although we may not be conscious of any specific personal need of our own when we pray together, another present may out of timidity or fearfulness be concealing one. Here it is well to be still — be quiet and wait a moment — until the Divine love present (Christ with and within all of us) enables the need to be brought into the open and healed.

At a recent conference we experienced this very thing. Eight people met daily to talk and pray about the small groups they were to lead following each message. After the second session, the need was suddenly revealed. Here is how it happened. I had asked them to stand in a circle, holding hands for a few moments while we prayed. I have discovered that a change in position brings freshness to our requests as well as to our bodies.

As we stood there, all taking part quietly, a professional woman of some renown, suddenly spoke to a retired missionary. "I can't stand in this circle holding your hand without asking your forgiveness. Nor can I any longer conceal our violent disagreement." There was mutual admission, forgiveness and God's healing love.

"As long as I didn't have to take her hand in prayer I could hide my hostility toward her," said the first woman, "but with the love active in this circle, I could no longer pretend. I had to let go — and let love take over."

When people pray aloud together, love is given and received, and there is the power of Divine love to heal. For Jesus Christ is love and He is healing. All healing love centers in and radiates from Him, and is directed to us whom He loves.

This is what Christ does. He draws the confused currents of human love into the unifying stream of Divine love.

Where Christ is present, in, among, and with His children there is healing- love and healing power present.

⌣

Jesus: If you knew what God can give, and if you knew who it is that said to you, "Give me a drink," you would have asked him, and he would have given you living water!

The woman: Sir, give me this water, so that I may stop being thirsty. . . .

Jesus: Drink this water I give, and you will never again be thirsty, for my gift will become a spring within your very self, continually refreshing and constantly fulfilling you — now and through eternity.

(John 4:10, 14, 15; based on Phillips)

⌣

～11～

Discovering joy in prayer

Isn't it wonderful to know how to pray, Ros? *Daily Light* for this evening has verses about asking in His name and *getting!* I've discovered that praying isn't a separate part of your spiritual life — it's your very life. It is God's presence. This is what "Christians" are always seeking to grasp, isn't it?

Prayer is problem solving. Prayer is getting back on good terms with Him — when we've let things get out of kilter.... And prayer is just daily *everything,* off and on, throughout the whole day. If you haven't learned how to pray, you're stuck! Thank you for showing me how to pray!

This brand new believer is not making a cut-and-dried method out of the four steps of prayer I taught her. She is making them serve to bring God into her everyday life and activities. Her joyous discovery is contagious.

Anna B. Mow, author of *Your Child* (and other books, Zondervan) constantly meets in her travels people who, having read my first book on prayer, started conversational prayer groups in their church, but have found them sometimes ineffectual. After a few questions, she discovers they are trying to follow a method instead of talking to Jesus as a person — in a spirit of love and freedom.

How do you get into the spirit of love and freedom when you pray?

How can I give you a formula for love? Or for freedom? Or even for prayer? I can only share with you what works for me, what has renewed me and restored to me the joy of living. Read again the two paragraphs at the beginning of this chapter. There is enthusiasm! There is discovery! There is freshness and newness. There is the presence of God and acceptance.

Why not begin anew as a little child, speaking from your heart to Jesus Christ who is present? After you've become at ease with Him, you will know when to address "Our Father," but do start with being as a child at the feet of Jesus.

We have already discovered that a child is both teachable and unself-conscious. Self-consciousness is an adult hurdle which presents a definite barrier. If one is aware of inadequacy in prayer-language, or of inexperience in audible prayer, or of inability to express himself in prayer, these become barriers of self-consciousness. Barriers when recognized can be broken down so that a new highway of expression can be prepared.

Four basic steps

The purpose of these four steps to prayer is to give beginners in prayer a place to start — a workable plan. They will serve as a pattern-breaker to replace previous attempts which ended either in failure or cold conformity. You will find the painful self-consciousness slipping away unnoticed as you begin to concentrate on the meaning of these four steps. To follow them requires your attention, and this in turn produces fresh interest.

1. Jesus is here. Matthew 18:19-20
2. Thank You, Lord. Philippians 4:4-7
3. Help me, Lord. James 5:13-16
4. Help my brother. Mark 11:22-25

Read them again. There are only three words in each step. Look away from the page now, and repeat them. You will never forget them, and you will find yourself following them at the most unlikely moment — which is the way prayer ought to be offered.

All you may have learned in your own private school of prayer can be fitted into these steps, and once you've used them, you'll find the order is not important. I am not trying to teach you a method. I am attempting to teach you to speak with a Person who loves you. These guide lines are intended to quickly and easily make the "how-to" part both familiar and workable.

You will find these four steps prepared in a brief outline at the close of this chapter. I have them prepared in convenient card form for prayer workshops. My publishers have given free permission to all wishing to reproduce them in mimeograph form for the purpose of teaching prayer, providing they comply with the following: Send one copy with your name, address, church (or group) to me, c/o Zondervan Publishing House, 1415 Lake Drive, S.E., Grand Rapids, Michigan, 49506.

Step by step

1. *Jesus is here*

There is no problem praying when God is near. To feel His nearness, you act on the knowledge of the truth of His presence. You will increasingly learn how to make use of your creative imagination. The Spirit of Christ will be there with you, whether or not you feel Him.

(For the leader: This is a time for silent worship, with participants centering on the thoughts you give them. Read Matthew 18:19, 20. A suggested opening is: "Hear the words of Jesus . . . (read the verses). Let us forget one another and remember we want to be as little children at the feet of Jesus." You may use other ideas or Scripture, but keep the meditation very short, very specific, suggesting *Christ with us,* here and now.)

2. *Thank You, Lord.*

The first step is the beginning of silent worship together. The second step is a continuation of worship in which all participate. Giving thanks is a form of worship which opens not only mouths, but hearts. Let your sentence prayers be brief. If you have two "thank you's" then pray twice, letting others pray too.

(For leaders: These first steps are a unit of worship in receiving love. The next two are a unit in giving love. You may have to remind them several times to give thanks for only *one* thing at a time. This, in the beginning, encourages many to take part who otherwise might remain silent.)

3. *Help me, Lord.*

At this time (God will guide you) you must decide whether or not you wish to admit a specific fault or need. If you do, those present will pray for you.

(For leaders: You will need wisdom and discernment when you introduce this third step. Much will depend upon those present. Sometimes the group needs to be broken into twos or threes for periods of five or ten minutes. If this third step is consistently omitted, a lack of personal honesty and healing love is fostered, and the result is a rather "cold" prayer time.

4. *Help my brother.*

As soon as a person prays for himself, another one or two should be applying a "band-aid" of love upon that wounded spirit. Any revealing of the heart calls for immediate response on the part of those who heard the prayer. Let your prayer-response be brief, to the point, with thanksgiving and with love. And without preaching or suggesting! Prayer should involve neither of these. We pray for each other by name, back and forth sometimes, according to the discernment received through listening and through loving. It is important that the group be small so first names — yes, first names — of those present are used. Prayer then becomes a more meaningful act of personal love and concern.

Joy is a gift

Joy in prayer is a gift which comes as a result of loving and being loved. Jesus said in John 15:9, 11, 12 (Amplified N.T.):

> I have loved you [just] as the Father has loved Me; abide in My love — continue in His love with Me. . . . I have told you these things that My joy and delight may be in you, and that your joy *and* gladness may be full measure *and* complete *and* overflowing. This is My commandment, that you love one another [just] as I have loved you.

As you continue to read chapters 12, 13 and 14, you will find further instruction on these four basic steps. We are simply outlining a fresh approach on loving one another as Christ has loved us, by praying together. We can consciously receive His love when we are consciously in His presence; then we have an abundant supply to give away. To learn to give love and care through praying together results in sudden joy springing up in all our hearts.

Our need to pray together

"I have just attended an abysmal prayer meeting," wrote a friend of mine. "Why people even bother to keep coming is beyond me. The spirit was lacking, requests were general, praise and thanksgiving almost nonexistent. The prayers were lengthy and oratorical. How can we be so insensitive to human need all around and within us by calling this a prayer meeting!"

After reading my first book on prayer, a concerned pastor wrote:

> My people need to learn to pray with one another. They need to discard old patterns of rigidity and traditionalism. They need to love one another in prayer. They need to be re-born, an experience which comes through prayer.

Do people who are unable to pray become reborn when they pray? Yes, they do. I found when I explain these four steps and announce a demonstration of them, people are eager to learn. I invite those desiring to participate to meet me after the lecture in a certain place. For five or ten minutes we stand together in a circle as I lead them into an actual experience of conversational prayer by following the four basic steps.

After one such demonstration, I received the following letter:

> My husband had been having trouble with his nerves due to the tension of starting a new business with his brother-in-law. For about 10 days before you came, he had been acutely miserable every morning. That Tuesday night after you spoke, my husband, daughter, and I stood in the circle. For the first time in his life, my husband felt the Holy Spirit

invade his soul and he spoke aloud saying only, "Thank you, Jesus, for the relief I feel." Following this came my husband's complete conversion. The next morning the three of us had our first prayer time together . . . aloud.

Do you wish to discover joy in prayer?

Open your heart willingly for Jesus to love you.

Follow the suggestions in this chapter.

And start praying now with one other person. If you don't know who that will be, ask God — He'll show you.

⌐⌐

True prayer is loving sensitivity.

⌐⌐

CONVERSATIONAL PRAYER

We Start with His Presence

(we receive His love)

1. *Jesus is Here* . . . . Matthew 18:19, 20
   Use creative imagination and silence.
   Visualize Christ. Welcome Him.

2. *Thank You, Lord* . . . . . . Philippians 4:4-7
   Gratitude is a heart-opener.
   Audible. Brief. To the point.
   Open-end prayer — don't close it.

We Pray for One Another

(we give love)

3. *Help me, Lord* . . . . James 5:13-16

   Forgive me, Lord . . . be specific.
   Pray for yourself . . . be honest.
   Then others can pray for you.
   Say "I" when you mean yourself.
   Say "we" when all present can be included.

4. *Help my brother* . . . . . . Mark 11:22-25

   Lord, answer his prayer! This is prayer-response.
   Pray for each other by name.
   The Holy Spirit will put into your heart what you
      should pray for.
   Pray briefly, informally, with love.
   Give thanks when someone prays for you.

This Is Love in Action

Love one another as I have loved you. John 15:12
Ask whatever you will, and it shall be done. John 15:7

This kind of prayer-from-the-heart is love in action.
We become involved in God's purposes, in His viewpoint, and with each other's needs for love's sake. Then
the circle may widen to include family, friends, church,
our nation, and the world.

by Rosalind Rinker
Author of *Prayer—Conversing With God*
(Zondervan, Grand Rapids, Mich.)

Part IV. Four Basic Steps in Prayer

⌣12⌣

The presence of God

— The first step: Jesus is here —

"Sir, we would see Jesus."

The request was made to the disciple Philip by certain Greeks who had journeyed far for this very purpose.

Jesus' answer to this request is found in John 12:23-27. Unless a kernel of wheat falls into the ground and dies, it remains a single kernel, but if it dies — it bears a great crop! Seeing Him in the flesh, He explained, is of little importance compared with seeing Him after His resurrection.

Hymn writers love to write about this theme — that moment when we shall see the Lord Jesus in glory with our own eyes. Why, I wonder, do they limit this moment to after death?

Each of us is influenced by mental concepts and preconceived ideas. Many believe they know what Jesus looks like. Others do not. The important thing, here and now, is not what Jesus looked like while on earth, but whether we are aware of His Presence with us.

Have you ever seen Jesus?

"Tonight in church," wrote a friend who had that day experienced forgiveness, "each time I closed my eyes, or looked at the wall or ceiling, I saw the Lord Jesus Christ. Not His face, just His arms and hands outstretched

99

to me. I couldn't stop thanking Him for His forgiveness, nor praising Him for being right there; for letting
me see Him; for wanting me to love Him. It is over-
whelming, that He loves me and wants me. I no longer
have to be afraid of Him, nor of myself. I've never before
felt this loved or accepted. For the first time in my life,
because I know God accepts me, I can accept myself."

The reality of Jesus' presence is not reserved for a
favored few, unless you call the "favored few" those
who seek Him. I was never too successful in realizing
the presence of God until my attention turned to Christ.
Only then did I believe and understand the words, *"Remember, I am with you always."* (Matthew 28:20,
Phillips).

The presence of Jesus *is* the presence of God. For
Jesus Christ is the image of the invisible God, God-with-
us — Immanuel. "The man who has seen Me has seen
the Father," Jesus explained to Philip, who could be satisfied only if Jesus would *show* him the Father.

"Everything in the Christian life depends on our having a growing sense of Jesus as a person," writes H. A.
Hamilton in the little classic, *Conversation with God*
(Abingdon). "We have to get to know Him in our minds;
we have to practice the art of living with Him. There
is no other way."

In my book on witnessing, I have already related at
length how I discovered Christ is not merely an experience, a plan of salvation, nor a part of theology, but
a vital, living Person, whose presence with us makes
possible two-way communication — communication filled
with response and meaning!

This discovery made it possible for me to ask Christ
to take possession of my mind, to help me develop

creative ideas which might help others not to be afraid to meet the Lord face-to-face — to see Him — to know Him — to believe Him — to feel His love and be assured of His acceptance and His forgiveness.

Jesus is here!

1. We must be aware of the difference between saying prayers, and knowing the nearness of Jesus Christ. The problem in prayer is not that of being taught how to pray, but being assured that God (who loves us) is always near and always with us, in the person of Jesus Christ.

2. We must be willing to be like a child: to come, to believe, to speak from our hearts, without self-consciousness, as we already learned in chapter 7.

3. We must not be afraid nor reluctant, for His love will hold us and heal us. If you are still fearful or unwilling, reread the first five chapters.

4. We must remember that our attention span is very short, especially when attempting to visualize the invisible. Our awareness of His presence will be quick, fleeting, but nevertheless real. As the Apostle Peter wrote, "whom having not seen you love," speaking of Jesus Christ. Cherish these moments.

5. We must speak to Him, and we must say His Name. "Lord Jesus, thank You for accepting me, just as I am." Strangely, there are people who are unable to say the name of Jesus in prayer. They can say, *Our Father,* but struggle when it comes to saying, *Dear Lord,* or *Lord Jesus* in prayer.

"This adventure in prayer," wrote a mother of four children, "requires a conscious effort on my part to speak the name of Jesus. Now, however, I know for a certainty *Jesus is here,* and that He loves me."

"This new concept of *Jesus is here* has changed my whole prayer life," writes R.D.B. of Texas.

"I must express my gratitude for introducing me to the living Jesus. There was a calm, joyous warmth radiating from each of you present, a certainty in your reference to Him, a sureness that His promises are true. I was eager to learn more about this invisible Visitor of whom you each spoke with such positive reference, that I, too, might know Him personally" (L.H.M.).

6. The secret of His presence is primarily one of awareness, of wordless wonder, and of communication — which enables us to exchange ideas as well as questions. We can respond, be assured, and feel a growing sense of security and reality in our relationship with Christ.

Creative imagination

We must let Christ speak to us.

In the other five steps I've suggested using ideas which will need some of the good creative imagination with which God has endowed you. In this step, I'd like to introduce an experiment, made by Frank Laubach, which I have tried and have found works. I have asked others to try it, and each time the answer comes back, "I tried it! And it does work!"

This requires more of the kind of imagination which precedes all progress. Read about it, at any rate, and do with it what you want and wish.

Dr. Laubach frankly admits this experiment borders on the mystical, but is nevertheless an experience everyone could and should have. Every Christian is, in a sense, a mystic, for we worship God Who is invisible, and speak with Him Who has no audible voice. Within the limits of our own personality and through this experiment we may know Christ speaking to us.

From the accumulation of your knowledge of Christ, His words, and His ways (which the Holy Spirit has promised to bring to us whenever we need it) we can best carry out this experiment while we walk alone, or are alone in a room. Let both sides of the dialogue come right out of your own mouth — and I mean in plain English!

The conversation might go something like this:

Mary: Lord Jesus, are You right here with me?

Jesus: Yes, Mary, I am here with you.

Mary: Your love for me never changes, does it?

Jesus: No, My love for you never changes; I always have and I always will love you.

Mary: But Lord, sometimes I'm a mighty mixed-up person. How can You love me? Most of the time I don't even like myself.

Jesus: I understand how you feel. Your insight about yourself is indeed limited. I, however, love you for yourself, and My love includes your total self — your *real* self, and all of your potential. Believe this for I am here to help you.

⌣

(For further exercise in the manner described here, read Meditation No. 4, then reread it aloud.)

⌣

Meditation No. 4

My child, I love you!

1. My child, I love you.

I love you unconditionally, good or bad, with no strings attached. I can love you like this because I know all about you — I have known you ever since you were a child. I love you and I know what I can do for you, and what I want to do for you.

2. My child, I accept you.

I accept you just as you are. You don't need to change yourself. I'll do the changing when you are ready. I love you just as you are. Believe this — for I assure you it is true.

3. My child, I care about you.

I care about every big or little thing which happens to you. Believe this. I care enough to do something about it. Remember this. I will help you when you need me. Ask me. I love you. I accept you. I care about you.

4. My child, I forgive you.

I forgive you, and my forgiveness is complete. It is not like that of humans who forgive but cannot forget. I love you, and my arms are open with love that asks, Please, come here to Me! I forgive you. Do not carry your guilt another moment. I carried it all for you on the cross. Believe this. It is true. Rejoice and be glad.

∽13∽

The power of gratitude

— The second step: Thank You, Lord —

In the last chapter I pointed out that sensing *God with us* is an individual matter. As we choose to act on our knowledge of the truth that God is always present, our minds and our emotions become involved and we say, "I feel the nearness of God."

Presumably, each person has had some private experience with regard to the presence of Christ, and some mental concept of what he believes Jesus' appearance to be. Because I remember vividly an old hymn from my early teens, "I shall know Him by the marks of the nails in His hands," my visual concept is not of His face, but of His hands and His feet. Seeing the scars (marks of love) I know Him, and my heart feels an inner enlarging and overflowing which is beyond description.

Just thinking of myself at the feet of Jesus, I am without words, lost in a sense of worship and gratefulness which seem to be pouring into, around and through me. The extent to which silent worship is effective depends upon our use and practice of meditation. Sooner or later, however, most of us will also need words with which to try and express our thoughts. Educational psychologists tell us nothing becomes a part of us until we have expressed it in words.

I hope, while reading this book, you have discovered my deep concern that people who live together pray together. Praying together in a relaxed, conversational, meaningful way brings real heart-communication with response — praying together and aloud.

You may recall the story of the family of three in a recent chapter who wrote me of their first audible prayer time together. Can you imagine this taking place in your home?

Audible prayer is never easy, for the simple reason we are extremely hesitant to reveal ourselves to one another, as praying aloud will do. I am not going to dwell on all the therapeutic and "releasing" aspects of audible prayer, except to say that when the "sound barrier" is broken and you begin to learn to speak to God in the presence of one or two others, great discoveries follow. You will find other people are a great deal like yourself. This discovery brings a new compassion for all men. Once you have become vocal and honest and personal, you will discover you are loved and accepted in ways not possible had you remained silent.

I recall a week-day audience in a Presbyterian church. They had been accustomed to silently taking part as their leader varied the program of the hour with worship material and the reading of requests, mentioning local as well as national needs. I was invited to share with them some of my own discoveries in group praying, as they wanted to learn new prayer techniques.

I'll admit I was a bit dismayed at the number present. If there had been 30 instead of 300, I could have handled it quite easily. Perhaps it was well I knew I couldn't.

It forced me to immediate prayer. I had planned to introduce them to the four basic steps. But what could I do in a practical way with 300 people!

As I stood there, the answer was there for me. We should do only the first two steps. I would take them into the meditation on the presence of God, then invite those wishing to participate to pray aloud in the second step, "Thank You, Lord, for _____."

I gave them a few simple instructions.

We would remain seated, and relaxed.

We would speak so those nearby could hear us.

We would give thanks for only one thing in one sentence.

We would not conclude these one sentence prayers with a formal ending.

If we had four items for thanks, we would remember that meant praying four times.

But we would also remember to give someone else an opportunity before we gave our second prayer of thanks, for this is the meaning of the words, "conversing together with God in prayer."

It is important that we continue to discipline our minds if we are to be conscious of the presence of Christ, for conscious worship will produce specific thanksgiving. Give Him thanks for what He has given, provided, made available — past, present and future. You are speaking *to Him,* not to people.

You don't have to "think up" something to say. As you keep your heart open to receive the love of God, you will find the words right there — speak up, say them, more will come.

The growing sense of joy in such a thanksgiving prayer service is so encompassing, I often wish we could tape what is being said, so those absent might share in our experience.

This particular service with 300 present "got right off the ground" immediately. People took part and the sentence prayers of thanksgiving began to surround and to penetrate us, to draw us together, to give us a sense of oneness, of belonging, of the love of God present. I heard some voices praying more than once, and I was glad, because the more often one prays, the easier honest expression becomes.

Then my attention was drawn to a couple on the front row. (I don't always close my eyes, but I do maintain an inner attitude of worship, and I do keep my inner eyes on the Lord Jesus.) This couple arrived late, and the only available seats were in the front row. He was a big man, heavier and taller than the woman. He began to fidget, tap his fingers, cross and uncross his legs — and I knew he wanted to take part in the prayer time. My silent prayer for him was answered.

He cleared his throat, lifted his head, and gave thanks.

"Dear Lord," he paused, and continued, "thank You — thank You for this swell wife of mine!"

Other "thank You's" went on and on, but as I looked again, I saw his hand on the back of the pew drop to her shoulder. She was fumbling in her purse, and brought out a handkerchief. Possibly it was the first time she had ever heard him pray aloud — and for her.

⤙

One woman who had long ago stopped attending prayer meetings because she did not wish to be embarrassed was persuaded to attend a small group meeting in a Kansas home. Telling me her story, she said, "I told them when I came in that I had not come to take part, but to listen. But when I heard how simply and honestly they prayed, like children with open hearts, I couldn't help myself. I was the third one to speak up and pray! I couldn't believe my own ears!" Since then she has become a member of a new group in her own neighborhood, and a whole new dimension has come into her life.

⌣

"Pray with these strange women I've never met? Never!" said a young mother to herself, as during a workshop on prayer, she joined a small group to which she had been assigned. "But I did," she continued happily, "and I found they were my sisters but I didn't know it. How rich I am now!"

⌣

One of the most remembered prayer meetings in my travels (and there have been many) was held in the basement of a large Mennonite church in Indiana. About 200 women were present, and I spoke on the four basic steps in prayer. Remembering the 300, I suggested we follow the same procedure by using only the first two steps. (The last two steps, "Help me," and "Help my brother," are often too personal for such a large number of people. These steps can be easily followed at home.)

The quiet, clear expression of thanksgiving seemed to weave a web which enclosed us with a sense of belonging — a sense of joy — and the presence of Jesus was real. For a whole hour they gave thanks — for people in their lives, for spiritual blessings and for material blessings; they even gave thanks for difficult situations which thrust them back in dependence anew upon their Lord. At the close of that hour, we sang with a new awareness for the familiar words:

> What a friend we have in Jesus,
> All our sins and griefs to bear.
> What a privilege to carry
> Everything to God in prayer.
>
> Oh, what peace we often forfeit,
> Oh, what needless pain we bear,
> All because we do not carry
> Everything to God in prayer.

We had been in His presence, we had touched Him with our words, with our faith. We had accepted anew all that life was bringing to us, knowing He was in it with us. We were refreshed and renewed in body, mind and spirit.

Have you ever tried it — just giving thanks?

Just give thanks, and leave the "asking" until later.

The practice of being grateful turns minds to new channels of creativity. It releases us from the bondage of ego by recognizing all gifts are from God; everything given in life creates an awareness of His lovingkindness.

⌣14⌣

The responsibility of love

—The third and fourth steps —

At the close of a lecture on prayer, a modestly attired little woman approached me, and asked if I would pray with her. Moving to a quiet, vacant corner, we sat down and together prayed. Afterward her gratitude was so apparent, I asked, "Don't you have anyone with whom to pray? There is a woman's prayer group in this church, isn't there?"

She assured me there was, but added it was not possible for her to take her request to them. The request concerned her sick mother living in Germany. This woman, an only child, was faced with making a decision concerning her mother — a decision too great for her to make without help. Again I asked why she couldn't share her problem with the group and request their prayers.

"You don't understand," she tried to explain, "they do not pray for themselves at their meetings. They do not pray for personal needs but rather for missionaries and world needs. I can't ask them to pray for me, as mine is a personal request."

How many times have we been in a meeting with other believers, feeling our very life being pressed out of us by burdens too heavy to bear? Did anyone know this?

111

Did anyone sense it? What provision, among all the various kinds of meetings for Christians, is made to assure love, concern and the sharing that helps lift burdens? Most of our "meetings" are too large, or too general, too social, or too public to encompass personal needs.

I've discovered it isn't necessary to make elaborate plans, nor schedule rooms in order to pray together. God's love, operating in our hearts, requires no pre-planning. Nor do we need advanced programming before stretching forth a helping hand to another.

At the close of another lecture, a lady said, "I'm one who has never been able to pray aloud. Can you help me, please?" I slipped my arm through hers. We turned from the gathering crowd, and suddenly ahead of us I saw a long hall. It seemed to be waiting for us to walk down it. As we walked, I prayed aloud,

"Thank You, Lord Jesus, because You love Betty. Thank You for bringing her here, today."

Continuing our walk, we prayed in short sentences. Because there was no strain nor artificiality between us, her "Thank You, Lord," prayers came as easily and naturally as my own. She was praying. She was thankful for what she'd learned and not afraid to say so. The joy was twofold because it was shared.

These two women illustrate the third step in our prayer outline — *Lord, help me* — *Lord, forgive me,* which is confession. Confession of need is often accompanied by tenseness and distress of some kind. For this reason, a fellow Christian can assume the responsibility of love by being there and sharing the need. When one prays for another, this is intercession. This is the fourth step: Dear Lord, please *help my brother.*

These two vital parts of prayer are very personal and

very necessary, whether performed alone or shared with another (or other) Christians. Here's how it was done with three working girls.

Three working girls

Two girls with whom I worked in China joined me in a decision to try conversational prayer — praying for one another. It was a first attempt and it wasn't easy, as our former prayers had been impersonal and general. However, we were determined to give this a day by day trial until we found out how it worked.

One morning before we met to pray, I knew I ought to begin to pray for myself, openly and honestly. I wanted my friends to pray with me and for me, using my name in their prayers. The previous day I'd felt a new depth of rapport between us when one of the other girls had prayed in this way. I decided my prayer would be one of admission concerning my strong tendency to be "bossy" — to always imagine my ideas are superior to those of others and far more workable.

"Lord," I began, "if I have been . . ." I stopped, sensing I was giving myself a "leg to stand on," which I really didn't mean to do. I started over. "Dear Lord, I sometimes have a tendency to . . ." I stopped again. I knew in that moment I was still not taking any personal responsibility for my actions and attitude. I started a third time! With determination. "Dear Lord Jesus, *forgive me* for always thinking my way is better, and for always wanting to 'boss' everything . . ." I stopped knowing I'd finally revealed the truth without rationalizing.

The girls were wonderful! They picked up this fragment of conversational prayer, with something like:

"Thank You, Lord, for Ros's honesty."

"Yes, thank You. We have always known she was like this, but it sure helps us to hear her admit it."

This brought a little subdued laughter, and ended our prayer. We looked at each other, and one of them remarked, "You know, it's funny, but this sort of honesty makes us love one another more. Why is it you love a person more when they admit a failure than when they just keep quiet about it?"

Praying with your family

This approach to prayer works very well in a family situation. It gives each member an opportunity to be themselves in the presence of God, without trying to cover up, which only compounds errors and further separates them from the very ones to whom they belong.

Here is a mother teaching her child to pray. Unknown to her, an experience that morning in a forbidden part of the neighborhood had been exerting pressure and guilt upon the child.

"Thank You, dear Jesus," prayed five-year-old Tommy, "that my Mommy didn't spank me this morning when I went into the cemetery, and help me not to crawl under the fence anymore."

Tommy succeeded in lifting several loads of guilt all at once. The mother thought twice, and prayed as honestly as he had. "Dear Jesus, help me . . . not to always be a 'spanking' mommy."

Here is a father and his 12-year-old son. "I don't seem to be able to get anything out of Carl," said the father. "He used to tell me everything. Now I don't know what he's thinking at all." The family began using the first two steps on prayer instead of the usual grace at break-

fast time: *Jesus is here,* then each one saying some meaningful *Thank You, Lord* prayer of gratitude.

I suggested that following their evening meal they try
the last two steps: Lord, please help me, and please help
my brother (father, mother, etc.). I also suggested that
one of the parents start it by admitting some fault of
their own. For as faults are admitted, in this mutual approach to each other's needs, and those present cover them
with a loving prayer, there is forgiveness and hard feelings
melt away.

A clergyman told me about teaching his family to pray
using these four steps. One Sunday evening he spanked
his youngest son, despite the child's insistence he was being
wrongly accused. Monday morning at the table, while the
family prayed conversationally, the truth came out, for it
is practically impossible to lie when one prays.

"Dear Jesus," prayed the little fellow, "thank You
for helping me to forgive my Daddy for spanking me
when I didn't do it." The father's honest prayer for forgiveness which followed healed a breach which could
have become permanent, and has separated many parents and children.

How it works in a group

Doris H. had come more than 100 miles to learn to
pray because she heard there was to be a prayer workshop. After brief silent worship, *Jesus is here,* we gave
thanks. Then as their leader, I moved to the 3rd step:
"Is there someone here who would like to pray aloud
for their need, so we may pray for you?"

Doris was the first. "Lord, forgive me," she prayed,

"for this resentment in my heart against a certain person in our church. I can't carry it any longer . . ." Quick tears cut off any further words. I wish you could have heard the women of that group "pick up her prayer" and in loving, brief prayer responses let her know they cared. So quietly and easily and with a bit of over-lapping did these prayers come that it was like a breath of fresh air touching us all.

"Thank You, Lord Jesus, for Your love for Doris."

"And Your love for the other person, too," added another.

"Thank You, Lord, for healing her now, from this inner resentment."

"Yes, thank You," came quietly from us all.

Doris prayed again, "I do thank You, Father, for Your forgiveness. I thank You . . . but . . . oh . . ." Here she paused before resuming her prayer; "Oh, I still don't love her, but I want to love her."

Again the group of women joined in "agreeing" prayer, expressed briefly and to the point as God's love flowed through them to Doris and even further — on to the other person concerned although she was not present. Space or miles are no barrier to the love of God.

Suddenly there was joy! All felt it at once. Doris, however, was the first to put it into words.

"Oh, thank You, Father," she prayed. "And thank you all for praying for me, and with me." Then I'll never forget her next words. "Now I can help pray for you, for my own burden is gone."

This is the meaning of bearing one another's burdens. To span the separation between us we can build bridges of faith and love, of caring and forgiveness for one an-other. We can give one another the comfort which comes through praying for one another by name. Another's courage to honestly admit a fault or express a need helps us discover we all fail and we all have needs. This human aspect draws us closer and tightens the circle of our love for one another.

About confession

1. You might like to refresh your memory on the first steps of confession found in Chapter 5.

2. If you are in a group, it is always safe to start on a surface level, with obvious things. By the response of your own heart and of those present, you will know whether it is the right time to move to deeper levels of need.

3. Honesty is an attitude which requires cultivation, so start now, and work at it. Let go of the image of yourself, and admit you often fail. The more specific you can be, the deeper will be the cleansing within you.

4. When you have learned to be honest, you will be ready to accept the honesty of another. Our acceptance of each other calls for trust and commitment to each other.

5. When any person admits sin, he is asking for and needs forgiveness. Don't withhold it from him, nor evade your responsibility of love by silence. Put yourself in his place. You will find that the healing of the heart comes from each of us to the other, as well as from God.

6. The problem of prayer-communication is not what the speaker says, but what the heart hears. You will never "hear" all that is contained in another's prayer until *you* have been honest to the point of pain. Having felt this, you will also feel the joy of the healing fellowship as others pray for you. Then your ears will indeed be opened to

"hear" with a new sensitivity, a new ability to withhold even your own request until another's has been met.

7. There is an immediacy about receiving, once we have asked, especially if our asking is done with the "agreeing" of those present and with thankfulness. Try giving thanks as you ask.

8. Are you able to face and name the areas of your differences? Are you ready to love and accept all people in your life?

9. Be on guard about exposing in prayer the sins of others. This is not an act of love nor of humility. Pray for yourself, confess your own sins. You do not need to criticize God's other children to Him when you pray — He knows all about them, and loves them as He does you.

⌐

> If we confess our sins, he is faithful and just to forgive us our sins, and to cleanse us from all unrighteousness.
>
> 1 John 1:9
>
> Confess your faults one to another, and pray one for another, that ye may be healed.
>
> James 5:16

⌐

⁓15⁓

Praying for others
Questions I've been asked

Question: Should we tell others we are praying for them? Wouldn't this embarrass them?

Answer:

I recall a group of about 30 elderly church women who discussed this subject after I had spoken to them on the responsibility of loving one another. They admitted they seldom asked for prayer for themselves, and rarely mentioned the subject to others.

To everyone's amazement, a white-haired woman in a wheel-chair spoke up, pointing her finger at a friend across the room. "When you were in the hospital those three weeks, I prayed for you every day!" She finished with an emphatic nod of her head.

"Well, for goodness sake! Why didn't you tell me?" replied her friend. "You could have told me on the telephone — you talked to me every day. It certainly would have helped my morale just to have known."

We take each other for granted too many times. Love must give the final answer, as to whether you will tell another you are praying for them, or whether you will keep quiet. While it might embarrass some, it will encourage others. There are many who never once in a lifetime have ever had anyone say to them, "John, I prayed for you last night."

One of the first meaningful friendships I made as a young adult came from telling another I was praying for her. A student from abroad, she had received a telegram notifying her of her father's death. It was Christmas vacation. Most of the students had gone home for the holidays. As I left the dining room that night, I stopped a moment to tell the girl I'd heard the news and that I was praying for her. Later, she told me I was the only one that mentioned her loss.

Question: Should we have prayer lists? They get so long; how can one know which names or requests to discontinue?

Answer:

If you mean a personal, at home, prayer list, do just as your heart plus your good common sense, tells you to do. I follow no methodical rules in private. Often, however, I write names down as I pray. This helps me to more specifically commit the person to the loving hands of my Father. I don't keep these lists. Instead, I start other lists as I feel guided to do so.

If you mean in a group — why not again use your good common sense? You select and choose in countless matters at home and at work. One practical word: whatever tends to staleness and boredom has outgrown its purpose. Keep finding different ways. Use your creative imagination. Ask and receive the wisdom God is waiting to give you. Or, invite another to share with you. Two agreeing — this is Jesus' pattern for asking and receiving.

Question: Would you discuss the subject of thanking God for a request just made but not yet answered? Can we give thanks before we have received?

Answer:

I certainly believe we can. In fact, Scripture encourages us to do this very thing. You should be familiar with Philippians 4:6, 7. Paul writes to encourage the Philippians to be careful about nothing — meaning, don't be anxious or worried. Instead, in everything as you pray, let thanksgiving constantly and consistently come through. The result is the peace of God, passing all understanding, keeping your hearts, minds and thoughts through Christ Jesus.

If we would practice this in personal prayer, and also in group prayer, how different might be our ability to believe and receive. Giving thanks is one of the highest forms of believing prayer. Giving thanks keeps one from excessive anxiety, and fosters trust. More and more I find myself praying with thanks, and if I forget, I simply start over.

Here is a short meditation I'll share with you.

I found myself praying:	*What I meant was*:
Go before me today.	Thank You Lord, for going before me.
Bless Denise and Lloyd (my sister and her husband)	Thank You, Lord for Denise and Lloyd. I see them now surrounded by Your love. Thank You for their love for me.

Help Denise in the prayer-group work opening to her.

Thank You, for open doors You've given her. Thank You, for filling her with insight, faith and love to do Your work.

Question: In order to believe you will receive what you have asked for, do you think making a mental picture helps?

Answer:

Yes, I do. Again let me give you Jesus' teaching on this subject from Mark 11:22-26. "Have faith in God. For verily I say unto you, That whosoever shall say unto this mountain, Be thou removed, and be thou cast into the sea; and shall not doubt in his heart, but shall believe that those things which he saith shall come to pass; he shall have whatsoever he saith."

The mountain represents the difficulty. Have you ever tried to imagine or visualize what a mountain dropping into the sea would look like? what it would sound like? what other results might follow? This is making a mental picture.

Here is an example of how it might work. In my travels last year, I spoke with a woman who longed to have her husband attend church with her. I asked how long she had been attending by herself? Her answer was — thirty years. I inquired if she had ever invited him to go with her? No, she hadn't, but she had wanted to.

"As we are sitting here quietly," I suggested, "think of yourself sitting in church. And now — think of your husband sitting beside you." I paused a moment and asked if she could visualize this. Could she form a mental picture of the two of them sitting together in church?

"Yes, yes, I can!" she exclaimed.

"This," I replied "is the joy of faith." Together we then gave thanks to God.

Later an unmarried woman, having heard of the above, asked me if she could pray for a husband in this same way. I told her I was sure there were many factors involved in her desire, things which needed careful examination.

Again, I repeat, God gave us common sense. If we don't know how to use it, then we certainly do need to pray with a Christian friend who does!

A young man who needed a job found himself stuttering and nervous each time he applied. We prayed together about this, and in our minds saw a mental picture of him applying without stuttering. He held this picture in his own mind the next day, applied — without stuttering — and got the job.

Question: For many years I've prayed that my daughter-in-law would become a Christian. How long should I keep asking? Should I give thanks, and leave my request with God?

Answer:

This is the one question I am asked more than any other. If your heart is not at rest about your prayer and about your loved one, keep asking. If your heart finds rest when you pray, give thanks and then turn the matter over to God.

Jesus taught us both kinds of prayer. The persistent, urgent prayer which finally got results is recorded in Luke 11:5-13. The prayer that brings joy with the answer is promised us in John 16:23, 24, where we are instructed to ask the Father in Christ's name. Joy is an immediate reaction. We don't *guess* we are joyful, we know we are joyful.

To you whose heart is not at rest, who keep asking — have you tried giving thanks? Also, are you cooperating with God? Is He communicating to you about your loved one? Sometimes God uses us to help answer our own prayers. Sometimes we hinder our own answers through ignorance or prejudice.

Heart-communication in prayer will bring rest. It will bring you guidance as to the next step of faith you must take — because *praying* is the first step.

I recall several years ago being with a small group of women, one of whom was actually weeping as she prayed for her daughter-in-law's conversion. After some talk and some prayer, we discovered she and the young woman were estranged over earlier difficulties. As soon as she began to give thanks and ask for ways to show love and forgiveness to her daughter-in-law, immediately great joy came to her. At that time there was nothing more to ask. There was now the carrying out of love in action which would be understood by the recipient. Yes, there will no doubt be other things requiring prayer attention before the final answer comes. These, however, God will reveal at the proper time.

A step at a time is the way faith progresses — that is, unless the mountain falls "kerplunk" into the sea in one mighty splash!

Question: Could you give our prayer group some fresh ideas or ways to pray for the problems of others?

Answer:

This book is already long enough. There are countless numbers of good, helpful books in print on the subject of prayer and prayer groups, with all kinds of helpful suggestions and techniques. You will find them on the shelves of any religious book store, or in your local library.

Here I have attempted to help individuals communicate with God and with each other, through love, and in prayer which is healing and freeing.

Verily, verily, I say unto you, Whatsoever ye shall ask the Father in my name, he will give it you. Hitherto have ye asked nothing in my name: ask, and ye shall receive, that your joy may be full.

John 16:23, 24